D0505945

JONATHAN

JONATHAN
An Autobiography

Jonathan Davies
with Peter Corrigan

Stanley Paul
London Sydney Auckland Johannesburg

For Karen, Scott and my family

Stanley Paul & Co. Ltd

An imprint of Century Hutchinson Ltd
62–65 Chandos Place, London WC2N 4NW

Century Hutchinson Australia (Pty) Ltd
20 Alfred Street, Milsons Point, Sydney 2061

Century Hutchinson New Zealand Limited
PO Box 40–086, Glenfield, Auckland 10

Century Hutchinson South Africa (Pty) Ltd
PO Box 337, Bergvlei 2012, South Africa

First published 1989
© Jonathan Davies and Peter Corrigan 1989

Set in Linotron Sabon
by Input Typesetting Ltd, London

Printed and bound in Great Britain by Mackay's
of Chatham PLC, Chatham, Kent

British Library Cataloguing in Publication Data

Davies, Jonathan
Jonathan: an autobiography.
1. Rugby Union football. Players – Biographies
I. Title II. Corrigan, Peter
796.33'3'0924

ISBN 0 09 174187 4

Contents

Acknowledgements

A sporting autobiography is usually compiled after the subject has retired and can quietly and unhurriedly reflect on his experiences. The story of this particular subject was written on the run, so to speak, much of it happening right before our eyes. Hence, it comes fresh – so fresh, in fact, that the rest of Jonathan's career is enfolding even as you read. The style we've adopted of describing each stage of his adventures with a narrative preceding his own words has enabled a large cast of voices to contribute to the story. We are grateful to his family and friends for so patiently recalling the dark and the bright days, and for the memory of his mentors such as Merion Davies and Brian Thomas. The players, the officials and the press men who have witnessed the drama at close hand have been very helpful, and only now will they realize how mercilessly their brains have been plundered. We wish that we could repay our debt to all concerned as lavishly as we acknowledge it.

The authors and publishers would like to thank the following photographers for permission to reproduce their copyright photographs: Colorsport, John Harris, Mike Brett, Eamonn McCabe/*Observer*, Express Newspapers, Alan Richards, Ryan Peregrine, *Llanelli Star*, *South Wales Evening Post*.

1
Crossing the Great Divide

Before Jonathan Davies had played his first Rugby League game he had worked out when he would play his last.

While others had been busy estimating how much he would earn from the record-breaking contract he received for moving from Wales to Widnes he was quietly calculating its expiry date.

'I make it May 1992,' he said from the back seat as, with his stepfather Ken, we drove back from Widnes after two hectic and bewildering days up there following his signing. The experience had absolutely exhausted him and we thought he was sleeping.

'What's happening then?' we asked.

'That's when I play my last game for them.'

'You haven't played your first bugger yet.'

'Yes, but that's when my contract is up. I can come home.'

To the many Welshmen who had greeted with horror the news of his move north their suspicion that he was a money-grabbing opportunist would have been confirmed. Having walked out on Wales and taken Widnes's money he was now planning when he could walk out on Widnes. But what we heard from the back seat was merely a symptom of severe home-sickness.

It was one of several strong and unfamiliar emotions that were to rush through Jonathan's arteries during that overwhelming time; the fixing of that date firmly in his mind was a great help in getting him through it. It is a device that works for soldiers and convicts too. But even that was no defence against the feelings that assailed him as he walked through a horde of jostling photographers to take his place on the Widnes bench as a substitute for the match against Salford eleven days after he signed.

For the first time in his life Jonathan Davies was feeling inadequate. As he stared at the game over the lenses of the photographers, who were by now sprawled along the touchline with their backs to the action, he felt completely stripped of all the brilliant qualities that had contributed to his world-wide fame as a rugby player and suddenly he was experiencing what the permanently inadequate know only too well – the fear of failure.

Happily it was a fear that stopped short of making him want to flee but not short enough to relieve him of acute discomfort as he watched his new team-mates engage Salford in the opening stages of a vigorous conflict into which he would soon be invited to present his credentials as the costliest player ever to cross that great divide between rugby union and rugby league.

Where now was the confidence of the truly gifted? Come to that, were his gifts still appropriate in this new game? And where had that other feeling gone, the one he was happy to let others interpret as arrogance, the self-belief that spurred him to explore gaps in the opposition lines that others couldn't even see, the cheekiness that led to the winks and blown kisses that so infuriated the much larger opponents deputed to smash him down?

It had all been steadily dissolved in the ten days since he had shocked the civilised world south of the Mersey by selling himself to the heathens north of it, an act that had led to him being called a defector, a traitor, a Judas even, for betraying his nation for an amount that varied in estimation from 30 pieces of silver to £500,000.

Once the trauma of making such a disruptive and irreversible decision had subsided and the shock waves of a media onslaught greater than for any previous league convert had passed by, there was still a long gauntlet to run before he could get to grips with his new career. It was a gauntlet manned more by the well-meaning than the malicious but there were so many determined to pelt him with advice and warnings, he was totally bewildered

Some of the advice had been invaluable, particularly from the men who were going to be alongside him, or preferably in front of him, in the Widnes side. Some advice he had deliberately sought like that of David Watkins, the great Welsh outside half who had made the same transition under almost identical circumstances 22 years previously and whose outstanding success made him a crucial man to be consulted.

The rest came whether he liked it or not. League stars scowled out of the sports pages under headlines prophesying doom, union men left behind scoffed at his chances, and sensitive commentators bewailed that his silky skills should be exposed to such brutality. Strangers came up to slide brotherly arms around shoulders they obviously considered too slight and wished him all the best with badly disguised shudders, others ran friendly fingers down the bridge of his long straight nose and urged him to have a last look at it in the mirror. Widnes had acquired the most talented half-back in the world and it appeared his achievements would be measured in how many days he could stay out of Widnes Hospital.

Much of it was good-natured but the sheer weight of it was colossal and although Jonathan laughed it off and handled the banter in disarming style, the cumulative effect was a gradual fading of a faith in himself that had been previously incandescent. In the end he had about him the resigned daze of a virgin being prepared for the bedchamber of a particularly rough Sultan.

Alongside Jonathan on the bench and unaware that his new player was plagued by greater anxieties than the usual plaiting of the intestines common to sportsmen and dental patients, the Widnes coach Doug Laughton was himself experiencing what he later admitted was an abnormal tremor. Signing Jonathan had been a spectacular coup but, as confident as he was that it was going to be very successful, he was appalled at the pressure the publicity had put not only on Jonathan but on himself and all concerned with the club.

'If I had known we were in for all this fuss and disruption I might not have bothered to sign him,' he said, jokingly.

Any hope he had of giving Jonathan a slow and quiet introduction to the game as he had done with the three union men he had introduced with great success during the previous 18 months – Martin Offiah, Scotsman Alan Tait and the Tongan forward Emosi Koloto – had been destroyed by the ballyhoo. It would still be slow but was doomed not to be quiet from the moment Doug announced his intention of giving him a run in the second half of the Salford match or 'earlier if one of our backs gets injured'.

What he didn't say was that if the game proved difficult and tight throughout and if he considered the inclusion of his raw recruit would do neither the player nor the team any good he would not put him on at all. With a crowd of 12,000, more than twice the average, craning their necks for a glimpse of the newcomer, over 100 pressmen representing newspapers from all over the world and more television cameras than you could count, Jonathan's non-

9

appearance would have been a lynching job but it was a decision Doug would not have flinched from.

After all, the most important product of the match was the two points they needed to maintain their challenge at the top of the League. The team did not deserve to be messed about for the sake of publicity. This hadn't been a case of signing a big-name reinforcement for a flagging team. In fact, if you'd made a list of all the major clubs in need of a star signing, Widnes would be on the bottom.

Their chances of retaining the Championship were considered inferior only to their chances of reaching Wembley for the Challenge Cup Final and few would have scoffed at their hopes of winning both. Jonathan had been signed not to replace anyone in Widnes's back division, and certainly not stand off Tony Myler who was rated the best in the business, but to supplement them.

All of which removed any urgency to throw him into the fray. Doug wanted to see him taste a little action but he didn't feel like being rushed. His cautious attitude was reinforced by the nagging knowledge of what had happened to two of the recent big-money signings from Wales who had been pitched into early action. Terry Holmes, the brilliant Cardiff scrum half, lasted just 13 minutes of his debut with Bradford Northern before aggravating the shoulder injury that was to ruin his league career. David Bishop, another brilliant scrum half of renowned toughness, finished his debut for Hull Kingston Rovers in hospital – and that was against Salford!

While Laughton tried to keep these thoughts buried beneath a close examination of a match that was taking a long time to swing Widnes's way, the person on the other side of Jonathan was also sensing an unaccustomed pressure which was not helped by the constant attention of the photographers whose motorised shutters fluttered noisily and greedily.

'How do you expect him to pick his nose with you lot taking pictures all the time,' she shouted at them impatiently.

It was not what you might expect from a young lady but then you wouldn't expect a young lady to be physiotherapist to a rugby league team. Viv Gleave is well used to people boggling at her role with Widnes and is refreshingly forgiving. In her two years at the club she has earned respect as a professional just like everyone else and the sight of her fair hair trailing in the wind as she races onto the field to attend to an injury has even ceased to activate any ribaldry in the crowd.

Nevertheless Jonathan was slightly unnerved by her presence in the dressing room and was certainly not prepared for her peals of laughter when she first saw him in a near naked state while noting his physical characteristics for her medical records. The first object of her hilarity were his arms. Since the bulk of Jonathan's weight and skill is based on strong quick legs and powerful hips, his upper body tends to lag behind in comparison and nowhere is his slimness more apparent than in his arms which are of the scrawny variety, especially when compared to the imposingly muscular limbs that dangle menacingly from most shoulders in the game. She instructed him to gain a stone in a month, the better to withstand the rigours of his new employment. 'And in the meantime,' she joked, 'don't lie on the beach, you'll get sand kicked in your face.'

Then she examined him and found the scars of his knee operations, discovered he was slightly asthmatic and diagnosed rightly that he had a slight curvature of the spine. 'You're a walking disaster,' Viv told him. 'And that's before you've even been on the field.'

And so it was that Jonathan sat on that bench, a stone under his newly declared fighting weight, shorn of the confidence his game depended on, beset by doubts about what he had let himself in for and trying hard not to transmit his nervousness to his two companions as he waited for that moment, 16.08 hours on Sunday 15 January 1989 to be precise, when Doug Laughton told him to get ready.

▽ J.D.

When David Watkins left Wales to join Salford in 1967 he was signed on a Thursday and was thrown into his first game the very next day, almost before he had time to draw breath, let alone study the rules. He tells me it was a terrifying experience.

Well, I waited 11 long days and lost 12lbs through tension before I got into the action. As I sat on the substitutes' bench waiting to go on in the second half I remember thinking – if this is the shallow end, give me the deep end anytime.

Not that I didn't appreciate the intention to give me a gentle introduction to the delights of rugby league but the build-up during those 11 days was such a shattering experience that the pitch became almost inviting. I say almost because so much had happened to my emotions during that high pressure period I began to doubt my own ability. I am always nervous before a game but never before have I feared making a fool of myself.

I had come up here to prove something, determined to show I was a good rugby player, a fact that my own country was beginning to doubt, and here I was as nervous as a kitten because of a sudden fear of failure, something I had never felt before. It wasn't my ability I doubted but my physical suitability for this new game which, I was assured, was like nothing I had ever experienced.

Since I had never been afraid before and considering that seven months earlier I was winning praise for flinging myself at the rampaging All Blacks, I don't know what I was worried about. It was just that my emotions had been put through a softening up process you'd have to experience to understand.

Making the decision in the first place was hard enough on the nerves but only those who have done it will really know how hard. The wrench of leaving home hit me with a force I hadn't expected. I found myself working out when my contract would expire, when I could return to my home village of Trimsaran. Having the date in mind seemed to help me cope with this hectic new scene but what really saw me through was that my wife Karen, baby Scott and Karen's mother came up with me from the start. We stayed at the Hillcrest Hotel to the north of Widnes where they made us feel very much at home. But it was being able to speak Welsh, my first language at home, whenever I could escape from the media which kept me in touch with reality.

But then I was aware of the constant questioning about my size and my ability to withstand the tackling. I kept insisting that I had no worries but they kept on saying that in league you get hit from a different angle, sometimes by two of them, that they roughed you up, that my upper body wasn't big enough to take the continual punishment.

In the end I felt that this was going to be a trial of my manhood more than my skill and that made me uneasy, so much so that I had to prove it all to myself as well as to them. So instead of easing my way in and sizing it all up, the pressure was on me to run around like a mad bull to shut them up. Only mad bulls tend to weigh more than 12 stone.

On the day before my first game Stuart Evans called in to see me. What a comforting sight he was. Stuart was at Neath at the same time as me; in fact I was captain and he was vice captain and since he was one of the best props in the world and 18 stone, he was always good to have about. We sat and talked for ages. He had come up to join St Helens 18 months earlier and had found the adjustment difficult. They say it is three times harder for a forward to make the change than for a back. But he'd had a cracking game the previous Sunday and he was feeling good about the prospects.

He said, 'You've got to stand up for yourself, because they'll be testing you right from the start. One of their tricks after they get you to the ground is to jab their forearm across the bridge of your nose and give you a bit of verbal.

'Just look them in the eye and say, "I can take that all day, you English bastard!" '

I thanked Stuart for this advice but said I'd probably think of something else to say, like 'Thank you'.

'And when you're running with the ball,' he went on, 'try to run towards a back instead of a forward, pick the man who's going to tackle you and pick a small one if you can.' It was sincere advice from a friend who had been through the action at the sharp end and I was delighted he was looking and sounding so positive about his future in the game after what had been a difficult start. But his words echoed through my mind – he had been one of the hardest and bravest men I'd played with and if he had been affected by the new demands, how would I fare?

Another former Neath player who had brought a mighty reputation into League was Glyn Shaw who had moved to Widnes from the Gnoll 12 years earlier and who is still playing in the Second Division. He had been a very successful convert and now has a thriving motor repair business in the town but he still remembered his debut and he recognised the doubts I was suffering from.

'When you play for great clubs like Neath or Llanelli and become a regular for Wales you're at the top of it all,' said Glyn, 'then you decide to go North and it is not until you are about to step onto a league pitch for the first time that you realise you're not on top any more, you're on the bottom. You are starting afresh in a different game with a totally new bunch of people to impress. It's a nasty feeling to creep up on you all of a sudden.'

There were other voices, less friendly and understanding. Kevin Ashcroft, the former Great Britain hero and now the coach of Salford, the team I was about to receive my baptism against, told the press: 'The pressure on Jonathan will be unbearable. He is bound to be affected. My team will definitely play on him and we'll find a few chinks in his armour. He is a brilliant attacking player but lacks upper body strength. My lads will run at him and test him in the tackle. We'll soon find out what he's made of.'

Garry Schofield, the player who went to Leeds for a world record transfer fee, gave little for my chances. 'There will be a special welcome put out for him. As soon as he touches the ball he can expect 60 stone of forwards piling into him,' he said.

Keith Jarrett, the boy wonder who came north in 1969, also wrote me off as not tough enough. Adrian Hadley, my Welsh team-mate who had gone north three months before, warned about the stick I'd have to take and cited the case of his Salford colleague Paul Shaw who was also a stand-off and had recently come over from Australia. 'Paul's a tough guy who has been around,' said Adrian, 'but he's been out most of the season with concussion!'

The warnings were endless and although most of them later claimed to have been misquoted, I decided not to read any more newspapers or answer any more telephone calls. But then came a call that cheered me up no end; it was from my sister Caroline to say that she and my brother-in-law Phil Davies, and Ieuan Evans and his girlfriend were going to drive up immediately after their match that afternoon.

Phil is the skipper of Llanelli and Ieuan, who is my best friend, their right wing and I couldn't have asked for more therapeutic company. But even mention of them brought more regret because it reminded me where I would have been that afternoon if I hadn't signed for Widnes. Llanelli were playing Neath at Stradey in what was virtually the Welsh club championship – and a game I would have dearly loved to play in as my last game. But Wales were playing Scotland the following week and I would have liked to have played in that too. If I had kept on looking at the fixture list I would never have gone.

Then I had another call, this time from my half back partner in the Welsh team, Robert Jones, to say that he and Paul Moriarty were also coming up with their wives immediately after playing for Swansea at Newport. It was with a happier heart that I went off house hunting with Karen.

I was considerably bucked up, too, when I managed to get the Welsh Channel 4 programme on the television set in our hotel bedroom and I was able to watch highlights of the Llanelli–Neath game with a Welsh commentary. Llanelli won, of course, with a great performance. Scrum half Jonathan Griffiths had an excellent game, as did the boy wearing the No. 10 shirt I had just vacated.

14

In fact Colin Stephens looked so much the part I felt as if I was watching a door slam behind me, with the one in the front of me still to be opened.

It was about then that the telephone rang and there was yet another of a long and flattering line of well-wishers. But this one was special – it was Terry Holmes whom I used to work with and who left Cardiff and Wales to try his luck in rugby league about three and a half years previously. I can well remember my feelings when he said goodbye, sad to be losing him but pleased at his decision. Nobody realised how little his career had left to run.

He wrecked his shoulder 13 minutes into his debut with Bradford Northern and although he went on to be a very popular player and personality in Bradford, he was never the rugby league great he should have been and the injury forced his premature retirement after only 40 games. Terry had been quoted in the press as advising me to watch out for the 'crazy gang' but he told me not to worry and was typically generous in his encouragement and his predictions for my future in league. But I couldn't get out of my mind what had befallen a player I had always looked up to as a rugby giant.

Any chance I had of returning to my earlier miseries was shattered when I was interrupted half-way through dinner by the noisy arrival of Paul Moriarty and Rob Jones. I greeted them like long lost brothers, even though I had played against Swansea the previous week in what was to be my last game for Llanelli. They had a good win over Newport to celebrate, particularly as Robert had made an excellent comeback after being ill with pneumonia.

I was catching up with the news when the Llanelli contingent arrived, a little late because Ieuan was driving and predictably got lost despite the fact he had spent three years at Salford University. They had plenty to celebrate as well and it suddenly felt very strange.

Here was Saturday night, the traditional piss-up time for rugby players, and here was I sipping nervously at a lager shandy while the lads were giving the Widnes beer a severe examination. But despite that I felt more relaxed than I had done all week. Not that there wasn't the air of a last supper about it, the gladiator's final night with the lads before his date with the lions.

It was midnight when I realised I shouldn't be there at all. The hotel was packed full and judging by the number who had come up to pass on their good wishes a large proportion of them would be in the crowd the following day. Although I had made a pint of shandy last all night they would be aware only of their new player

15

whooping it up at the rowdiest table in the place. It would not sound good if anything went wrong the next afternoon. So I said goodnight to my companions and it couldn't have been a more solemn farewell if it was a firing squad I was facing next day.

I didn't sleep much, in fact I'd have been less tense if I'd stayed down with the lads. Normally, not even the prospect of a vital game will prevent me having ten hours of serious shuteye but I lay there with the whirlwind of the past ten days rewinding through my mind. I could still hear the faint and muffled sounds of merry-making two floors below. Mercifully I must have nodded off before Robert Jones decided to do his Tom Jones party-piece.

Next morning I slept late and would have slept even later but for the ringing of the telephone. The hotel switchboard had orders to stave off all callers but Doug Laughton is not easily staved off.

'There's been a change of plan,' he bellowed heartily into my slowly awakening ear. Oh God, I thought, he's going to put me on from the start. My stomach turned somersault.

But all he wanted was to rearrange the time for me to pick up the club tracksuit. 'All going well,' he said, 'we'll put you on during the second half. But if one of the backs gets hurt, you'll be on a damned sight quicker.'

I was in the lobby trying to force a ham sandwich into a stomach the size of a walnut when the next carload from South Wales turned up. It was Bleddyn Bowen and John Devereux and their wives. It really was tremendous of them to turn up to give me a send off, particularly as no-one knew how long I'd be on.

On match days the team always gather at the Hillcrest to have a chat about the game and watch two or three videos of the opposing team. While I was getting engrossed in the opposition I suggested to Doug Laughton that he had a look in the hotel dining room.

The sight of the six Welsh internationals who'd come up, tucking into lunch on his own patch, was a rugby league coach's dream. 'Go and get the forms, quick,' joked his chief scout Eddie McDonnell.

When the lads got to the ground they were ushered into the stand and the tannoy informed the crowd of their presence. They were made to feel like visiting royalty.

Meanwhile, the team had left the hotel and had made the five-minute journey to the ground. As I nervously walked towards the changing rooms, I saw many old school friends and people whom I hadn't seen for years, shouting their support. To them this was alien as well.

The dressing room was quieter than I was used to. In union dressing rooms, or at least the ones I had been in, the atmosphere is far more urgent and noisier. Before a big game the voices would be louder and more aggressive as players psyched themselves up, even punching the walls as part of the geeing up process. It was a difference I was to analyse at greater length later but this first experience fascinated me because of the calmer, more businesslike way the Widnes players prepared for the game; talking quietly while having their ankles, wrists and thumb-joints bandaged as a precaution against sprains. It was as if they'd come to work and they didn't need anyone to tell them how important it was.

They were conscious of me and did their best to reassure me that everything would be all right, that when I came on I should listen to them and not go looking for the action. It would come to me soon enough and when it did I would know what to do. Just keep your eye on the man you are detailed to mark and not let him go past you with the ball and everything would be all right, they said.

It was all very matter-of-fact and very impressive and I felt better until I walked through the wire cage that covers the players' tunnel and out onto Naunton Park.

Since I have played on most of the world's great rugby stadiums before crowds of 60,000 or more, I was not about to be overwhelmed by the 12,000 packed into the Widnes ground. Yet my nerves were shrieking like a car alarm.

For a start I had never seen so many photographers in my life. I could barely see the pitch as this great horde walked backwards in front of me as I made my way to the touchline bench. As I passed the main stand, somebody burst through their ranks carrying a green and black Trimsaran shirt. It was Ken Ford, one of the two busloads of people who'd come up from my village, and a reassuring sight as he walked alongside me, waving the shirt at the crowd who were probably wondering what the hell it was.

As I took my place on the bench the photographers draped themselves on the ground between me and the pitch. Even during 11 days of what seemed to be non-stop clicking I still felt kindly disposed towards the cameramen but they were starting to get to me. There must be a limit to the number of interesting pictures you can take of a man sitting on a bench but they didn't seem to think so. What annoyed me more than anything else was that they had their backs to the game. Considering that Widnes were one of the top sides and I hadn't even proved I was good enough to become part of them, it was an insult to concentrate on me and ignore them. It certainly didn't make me feel any better about the pressure I was under to do something to justify all this attention.

I tried hard to concentrate on the game and watched Salford get off to a good start. They had beaten Widnes at home earlier in the season and were obviously intent on doing the double. I was obviously taking particular notice of their two recent ex-union men, England international Peter Williams and my former Welsh team-mate Adrian 'Adolf' Hadley. Adolf had the hardest job that afternoon because he was up against our star winger Martin Offiah who had already convinced me in training that he was the quickest thing in rugby boots.

Adolf managed to score a try but Offiah scored four in a breathtaking performance which, some of the press pointed out next day, stole my thunder. Well, thunder is hardly the word that best describes my entry into rugby league – a quick flash would be a more apt summing up.

It might have been different for both me and Martin. After 15 minutes he scored his first try, kicking the ball towards the posts and racing after it to touch it down as he crashed into the foot of the upright. Naughton Park erupted but Martin remained where he was, his face to the ground. The thought that my time had come prematurely rushed into my mind as Eddie McDonnell and Viv Gleave scuttled over to see what was wrong. It seemed a long time before Martin was helped to his feet and pushed groggily back onto the field. I have to admit that my pleasure at seeing him back in the action was not totally unselfish.

Gradually the boys were getting the upper hand. Joe Grima scored a good try and then Mike O'Neill made it 18–0 before Peter Williams got a try for Salford. It was a good game and the player who impressed me most was Tony Myler, probably because he was the one I was watching closest. Tony was rated the best stand-off in the league game and the reason most experts reckoned I'd have to get into the team in some other position. But in this match, Tony was playing at loose forward and he seemed to have it all – speed, handling skills, deadly tackling and the ability to read a game that led to a great try just before the interval.

By half-time the game was as good as won for Widnes and in the dressing room I was feeling slightly surplus to requirements and also embarrassed that if I was going to get my promised try-out one of the team was going to have to come off, and there was no player remotely deserving being yanked off for my benefit. Rick Thackray, the opposite winger to Martin, did have an arm injury that was worrying him but Doug told him to see how it went, and anyone searching the Widnes team for a clean white shirt as they trooped out for the second half would have been disappointed. I was still in my tracksuit.

The half was only four minutes old when Tony Myler went crashing through on one of his surging runs. He was tackled awkwardly and both he and the Salford man went down with their legs locked. You could tell by the actions of the players nearby that something serious had happened. The stretcher was soon being signalled for and as Tony was being lifted gently onto it with what turned out to be a broken left ankle, he looked up at one of the Widnes officials and said, 'It's a good job you bought Jonathan!'

At that moment Jonathan would not have agreed with him. The other substitute, David Marsh, was sent on to take Tony's place among the forwards, while I settled back onto the bench to await a call that might not now come.

As I strained to absorb as much of the game as I could, I don't think I would have minded had my debut been delayed until another day, but then came the moment. It was 12 minutes into the second half and Rick Thackray scored a superb try, sending two defenders the wrong way and then powering for the corner. Even as the crowd was celebrating a great score Doug signalled for Rick to come off and I was told to get my tracksuit off.

Rick ran across the pitch to well deserved applause and as I waited at the touchline I held out a nervous hand not quite knowing how he was going to take my replacing him. He knocked the hand away and gripped me in an embrace that almost broke my ribs. 'All the best, JD,' he roared in my ear. The ref waved me on, the linesman shouted 'Good luck' and I was on the pitch, taking a welcoming handshake from Joe Grima and running to a spot in the Widnes line that everyone was pointing to.

Andy Currier had moved out to take Rick's place on the right wing and I was going to play centre. The next 20 minutes were among the most bewildering I've ever spent.

The grass was the same colour, the ball the same shape, and the posts were familiar but the rest of it was so confusing it was like I'd been parachuted into a game I'd never seen before. I'd been through move after move in training, watched about 20 videos, asked 100 questions but I still wasn't prepared for the real thing.

Every instinctive, automatic move my years in union had pro-
grammed into me seemed to be wrong. League players change position continually, a lot of the time while running backwards, and
the newcomer finds himself continually becoming the one piece that
won't fit into the jigsaw. The boys were bellowing advice as fast as
they could: 'Over here, JD', 'Back off', 'Go now', 'Watch the offside'.
I managed to keep my bearings because of an opponent. Man-to-
man marking is essential in league. You pick out your opposite
number and watch every move he makes when they've got the ball.
Whoever else gets past you, he mustn't.

Luckily my opposite number was Peter Williams, someone I knew,
and wherever he was in their line I made sure I was between him
and our goal. What with following him and listening to my team-
mates I felt giddy, but not as much as my friends in the crowd, most
of whom were seeing a league match in the flesh for the first time
and were having a difficult time fathoming out what I was up to. If
I hadn't had the only clean shirt on the pitch, they said they might
have lost me altogether.

As for the ball, I never looked like getting anywhere near it. The
boys were trying to let me get my bearings before they introduced
anything as complicated as the ball into my thinking. Whichever
side of the heel I lined up on, they played it the other way. This
went on for ten minutes and I was feeling more like a formation
dancer than a rugby player.

I was desperate to do something, to stop feeling so helpless. All
of a sudden there was a Salford player heading for my section of
the line. I looked either side of me. 'Is he mine?' I thought. That
fear of making a fool of myself made me hesitate, and even half a
hesitation is fatal. By the time I had made my mind up to tackle
him, he'd gone past. There was a heartening crunch as one of my
colleagues did the job for me and mercifully the crowd decided to
overlook the matter.

The play ebbed away from me again, to the other side of the field
where Martin Offiah took a pass inside our half and made the
quickest run for the line I've ever seen. He spent the last 20 yards
looking back and holding the ball out teasingly to the unfortunate
Adrian Hadley who was pursuing him.

It was a tremendous try and as we all trooped back into our half,
a voice from the stand shouted, 'Well played, Jonathan'. It was all
good humoured but I felt that the need to make a contribution to

the game had become urgent. But the boys seemed quite content to keep the game away from me for what seemed like ages.

And then it happened. Salford broke on the right and there was no mistaking it this time. A large forward named Ian Blease was bearing down on me like a double decker bus. Doug had advised me to wear a light pair of shoulder pads. They felt strange but they cushioned the impact of bone against bone in the head-on tackle and at that moment I was grateful for them. I went for the Blease knees, so to speak, and down he went, dropping the ball as he hit the ground which everyone on our side seemed pleased about. It was just an ordinary tackle, like hundreds I'd made in union but none had made me more relieved. I felt like kissing Ian Blease but the look on his face was not that of a man happy to be sharing this historic moment with me.

From then on everything went smoothly. Martin Offiah scored another great try and Emosi Koloto bashed through to create a great opening for me. I just went, side-stepped one tackle, accelerated past another and as the third tackle loomed up I grubber kicked ahead as he bundled me into touch. The crowd made the sort of noise which suggested that they were as pleased as I was that I could still run with the ball.

I got far more involved in the last ten minutes and might even have scored a try as I chased after Alan Tait when he made a great break down the field. He kicked ahead and pounced on it for a touchdown. If he'd kicked it a little to the right I could have scored it, but you know how mean the Scots are.

The next thing I knew I was surrounded by swarms of small boys. The game was over and I was disappointed. I had survived the ordeal I had been dreading and I didn't want it to end. The elation was unbelievable. There were many bruises and blows to come in the weeks ahead, but I had become a rugby league player, and an intact one at that, and now I hoped the spotlight would ease a little and I could get on with my new career.

2

The Boy From Nowhere

Two coachloads had travelled to Widnes from Trimsaran, and a
large fleet of private cars from nearby Kidwelly, Carmarthen and
Drefach had swelled the number of hometown fans making the long
journey to about 100.

'Best to allow a good four hours and we'll need to be there by 12
noon to park in the club car park,' said Jonathan's stepfather Ken,
who had been to Widnes with him the previous weekend and had
been appointed consultant to the expedition.

In the end they allowed five hours – which is just as well for they
got lost around Birmingham – and that meant leaving at 7am when
the dawn of a mild January morning had scarcely lit the sky over
Pembrey mountain. They gathered outside Trimsaran RFC clubhouse and settled into the familiar upholstery of the coach company
whose premises are next door – a convenient juxtaposition because
Jonathan's big-match appearances for Neath, Llanelli and Wales had
regularly called for the bulk transportation of a high proportion of
proud villagers.

In fact, one coach had departed the previous evening. About 20
had decided to travel up to Widnes early and sample the local
Saturday night atmosphere, getting accommodation where they
could, three here and a couple there, in pubs and bed-and-breakfast
places.

The main party of 45, including Ken and Jonathan's mother
Diana, were on the Sunday morning shuttle and reached Naughton
Park at around noon. They were welcomed by Widnes secretary
John Stringer and promptly made honorary members of Widnes

22

RLFC Social Club, an honour they immediately celebrated at the bar.

As had been previously discovered by parties of Welsh rugby fans who have journeyed to the forbidden land of the league to cheer on a departing son, the two sets of supporters quickly fall into an easy and affable affinity. The chasm between the amateur code of union and the professional league goes deeper in many areas than mere discrepancies between the rules and the acceptability of cash rewards. There is a gap in class and social attitudes that would keep the games apart even if all else was reconciled. That gap does not exist between the industrialised regions of South Wales and the north of England. They wouldn't dream of exchanging games but they recognise a kindred nature in their love and appreciation of rugby of whatever brand.

Before and after the game they drank and joked and argued shoulder to shoulder in the Social Club bars which were packed to discomfort not only because of the abnormally large crowd but because one of the bars had been commandeered to house the 100 press people Jonathan's debut had attracted. So Trimsaran and Widnes men and women found themselves allied by their dislike of the media they could see supping in comfort as well as by their common interest in Jonathan's success in his new career.

That aspect of their new friendship was considerably more relaxed once the game was ended and he had overcome the first hurdle of this transition with enough credit to satisfy both old and new interests.

Reunions were planned, a match struck between Trimsaran Over-35s and Widnes Over-35s under union rules, and an act of charitable generosity occurred that they still talk about in Trimsaran.

A ball autographed by the Widnes players, including Jonathan, was raffled and won by a Widnes supporter. One of the visitors, a barber from Pembrey, offered £20 for the ball, explaining that he wanted to raffle it for a collection he was organising for the family of a local soccer player who had died of cancer. The offer was refused. Instead of money the Widnes man wanted four Trimsaran RFC ties. Within seconds they had been torn from the necks of their owners, smoothed out and handed over in return for the ball.

There was only one sour note. At the end of the bar was a stage and a microphone and when Pat Burke was urged by his fellow Trimsaran men to step up to it, a Widnes voice proclaimed, 'Oh Christ, they're going to start singing.'

But this was not to be a hymn-bashing session for which the Welsh are either renowned or feared, depending on your tastes. Some time before, Pat Burke and Jonathan were at a New Year's Eve party and pledged themselves to the usual ridiculous resolutions. Jonathan was going to play for Wales at the Arms Park and Pat was going to sing at a packed Albert Hall. Pat has yet to grace the Albert Hall but he has won a Tom Jones sing-alike competition on BBC Wales and the song with which he quietened the Widnes RLFC Social Club was quite appropriate. It was called 'The Boy From Nowhere'.

▽ J.D.

I get a little upset when people say they have never heard of Trimsaran, as they usually do. It might be easier if I said I came from Llanelli but sometimes even that fails to register, so I tend to simplify it all by saying, 'I'm from Trimsaran, which is near Llanelli, which is not far away from Swansea.'

To be exact, Trimsaran is five miles over the mountain from Llanelli. It is a mining village on the western edge of a coal-field that produced the finest anthracite in the world. Because it is the centre of *my* universe I can't understand why so few people are aware of its existence.

Everyone feels something special about the place of their birth but Trimsaran means much more than that to me, even more than the Welsh traditionally feel for their home at a time of *hiraeth* (homesickness). I look upon Trimsaran as an extra parent.

When my father died in 1976 he was 43 years old and I was 14 and, in the sad and confusing months that followed, Trimsaran seemed to take over a fatherly role in my life. Nothing was said; it was as if the men of the village took on a silent guardianship of my interests, creating a protective cocoon while I came to terms with the sudden gap in my life.

My mother, Diana, shepherded my sister Caroline and me through the hardships of that time with the same strength and spirit that had eased my father through his long illness. But the other influences necessary to help a 14-year-old develop in a normal and correct way were discreetly applied during day-by-day life in the village.

When my mother remarried I was very fortunate in her choice. Ken Williams, a Trimsaran man born and bred, had experienced his own tragedy. His wife Phyllis, one of my mother's closest friends, died at the age of 29 from leukaemia leaving him with a son, Peter, who is a few years older than me.

The joining together of the two families had strengthened everyone concerned and was of particular benefit to me. Ken brought the close support of a father at a crucial time and that's how I think of him now. Obviously I will miss my father for the rest of my life and bitterly regret that he hasn't been able to share in the success he wanted for me but I don't feel deprived because Mammy and Ken have done so much to compensate.

It was not, alas, the end of the tragedies. Another man who had given me great encouragement and support was my father-in-law Byron Hopkins. I knew Karen for a long time before we got married and watched him suffer from kidney trouble for years before he had a transplant from which he made an excellent recovery. But five years later he collapsed and died from a heart attack while we were all having a meal. He was 49. Before I met Karen he had little interest in rugby but that changed and one of his ambitions had been to see me play for Wales. I was picked to make my debut against England in 1985 just a few days after he died.

The ability to withstand so much grief and help others to do so comes, I am sure, from the strength I drew from Trimsaran's way of rallying to the rescue. I might not have recognised it then but I do now, and I still feel very strongly that extra sense of belonging whenever I go back.

It wasn't because I was anyone special. I was just one of the cheeky youngsters who made a nuisance of themselves. My rugby potential earned me little more than the description 'tricky little bugger', and there were plenty of those around. But I was one of theirs, part of a working community who have served the coal-mines and steelworks for long enough to know how to help absorb the shock of a prematurely taken father.

And it helped, of course, that my father was Len Davies. He was not a Trimsaran man. He was born in Llwyn-hendy, the other side of Llanelli, but was married to a Trimsaran girl and had highly acceptable credentials as a rugby player. He played centre for Swansea, then Llanelli and then Trimsaran for whom he was a very popular captain.

He was not tall and not particularly sturdy but he was very quick and when he had the ball in his clutches he was a very elusive runner. According to some shrewd judges I am neither as quick nor as nimble as him. I am just happy to have picked up enough of those attributes to get by.

But although my sister Caroline, who is two years younger than me and married to the Wales and Llanelli forward Phil Davies, is reckoned to be more like my father than me – I tend to show my feelings a little more forcefully than he did or she does – I follow him in one particular respect. He hated to lose and I'm not all that fond of it either.

I am sure that most people don't like losing but with my father it was a passionate hatred. Ken tells me that this was not only displayed on the rugby field, where one or two notable last-minute wins were achieved because of his refusal to accept defeat, but in less vital pursuits. If he lost a friendly game of darts he felt he should have won he was prone to go straight home, leaving his unfinished pint on the bar.

It was a habit I inherited from him and which brought me a lot of anguish because he never once let me win at anything, whether it was draughts, snap, snakes and ladders, blow football or sprints along the beach. He wouldn't dream of cheating but he did me no favours either, and he instilled in me a competitive spirit I wouldn't be without.

Unfortunately it has got the better of me now and then. I remember once throwing a tantrum after an adult team from Llandovery beat Trimsaran Youth in a sevens tournament. I was so enraged I kicked the ball into a tree. The referee made me climb up and fetch it. I learned the lesson – I'm still a bad loser but I don't show it.

As for inheriting his speed, I did that without realising it. At my first press conference after joining Widnes I was asked how it was I was so quick. I said, 'My speed comes from fear,' and they all roared with laughter and wrote about how witty I was. But I wasn't really joking. I assumed they wanted to know if I had been a good runner, had trained as a sprinter. But I never had a name for running fast in school sports. I was always second in the cross country to a boy called Jenkins and although I was always there or thereabouts in the sprints I was no faster than a lot of my friends.

Mammy was a very quick runner and when we used to have family races on the beach, my father would come first, Mammy second, me third and Caroline fourth and crying. I was 14 years old before I won a race against my mother, so I certainly didn't grow up full of confidence in my running ability.

But when I had a ball in my hands on a rugby pitch people said

I ran like the wind. Maybe it was fear. I was invariably the smallest and the incentive to avoid being caught was considerable. But whatever the reason, I seemed to be quicker with a ball than I was without it.

Not that I was ever far from a ball. By the time I had reached the toddling stage my father's first class career as a rugby player was over and he was captain of a very good Trimsaran side who played in the renowned West Wales area, so there was plenty of time to play with me. I can't remember him bombarding me with advice but he did bombard me with the ball. All he wanted me to do was to enjoy playing with a ball, any ball. Soccer ball, cricket ball, tennis ball – we played with them all for hours.

Whenever he played I was a ball boy and when I wasn't chasing after the match ball I had my own to kick and catch and throw. Gradually, the ball became an extension of me and I felt completely at home with it. I still feel like that today. I'm not always sure which way it is going to bounce as I'm chasing after a kick-ahead but I'll bet my guess against anyone else's.

It was this feel for the ball that was my father's greatest gift to me. Cluttering the minds of children with theory and advice is not the best way to bring out their natural ability. He believed in coaching but first of all he believed in letting the ball work its own magic on young minds.

My young mind first came to grips with the next lesson – that the world is full of bigger people who want to take the ball off you – on the patch of grass that runs in front of numbers 155 and 156 Garden Suburb, a council estate built in the 1920s when Trimsaran needed to house the labour force required for the village's two mines and for the nearby steel and brick works.

It was still a thriving area when my mother and father were married in 1960, so much so they couldn't find anywhere to live in Trimsaran. They moved into rooms in my father's birthplace Llwyn-Hendy which was convenient because it was nearer the Trostre steelworks where he worked in the buying department and also nearer to Swansea where he was playing.

But the pull of Trimsaran never relaxed its grip on Mammy and when I was due two years later she was installed in her mother's house at 155 where I was born on 24 October 1962. Fairly soon they got their own place in the village and eventually moved next door to my grandmother's at 156.

As a place to be brought up I can't imagine anywhere better. The description 'council estate' may conjure up all sorts of visions these days but down at the Garden Suburb things are just the same now as they were then, quiet, friendly and comfortable. The houses themselves are neat and roomy, the back gardens are narrow but long enough to practise sprinting and, being on the slope of the mountain, the views are far and clear. And not only are neighbours loved, they are trusted. At Mammy's house the key is in the latch all day and Ken never bothers to lock the car parked at the kerb.

Each house has a small lawn in front and since there was no fence between ours and my gran's next door it passed as suitable for games of two or three-a-side between six-year-olds. It was there that the first game-plans were born and executed. But the pitch shrank as we grew and matters came to a head when I broke the nose of a visitor from Burry Port with a high tackle that would now get me ten minutes in the sin bin. When his parents demanded an explanation my father said it must have been a lucky punch, which didn't go down well.

So we moved to new fields where the self-organised mayhem continued, not only in rugby but in soccer and cricket. Even at school we ran our own games because the headmaster of Trimsaran Primary didn't have a school team. But that all changed, and probably my life with it, when Meirion Davies arrived to teach at the school. Meirion, a very nice man, had played for London Welsh, Cardiff and Llanelli and immediately set about organising a school team to compete with others in the area.

His influence over a bunch of boys whose attempts at rugby had been undisciplined and instinctive was considerable. As a seven-a-side team we quickly became the undisputed champions of the area. As I was less than nine years old he asked permission from my parents to play me in the full school side in the Under-11 League and for me and my friends it was a time of sheer bliss.

When you read the life stories of star players you very often find the strong influences of a schoolteacher. Meirion Davies certainly comes into that category. Players like Nigel Davies, Andrew John and Carl Bridgewater were schoolmates of mine who went on to shine in first class rugby. Meirion just wanted us to play naturally, as we had always done, while he moulded us into a team, a team good enough to beat far bigger schools.

Small as I was he made the best use of my speed and my love of handling the ball. He discouraged kicking as an easy option and encouraged a sense of adventure, a willingness to try the unexpected, that I still think I possess today.

It was a great time but one that was to come to an abrupt end when I passed my 11-plus. Youngsters are supposed to be happy when they qualify to go to grammar school, but I was devastated. Most of my rugby playing friends hadn't passed the exam and so were due to attend Stradey Comprehensive, where Mammy had gone, a school close by Stradey Park, the home of Llanelli RFC, and the one I had set my heart on.

The school I was allocated to was Gwendraeth Grammar, which has a record of producing rugby players second to none in the UK. It was the school my father had passed for but couldn't go to because he was looking after his mother. It had a tradition of producing great outside halfs – the 'outside half factory' it was called. The great Carwyn James went there, as did Barry John and Gareth Davies, whose place in the Welsh team I was eventually to take. But I still didn't want to go there. I wanted to be with my friends. My worst fears were realised when I turned up for my first day. Karen Hopkins from Cefneithin, who was to become my wife, was another new pupil that day but I was much less interested in sharing a classroom with girls for the first time than I was in being robbed of my friends.

It probably went a lot deeper than that. Being small and skinny is no great advantage anywhere but in Trimsaran my ability at rugby had helped me become a bit of a hero. At Gwendraeth I was small and skinny *and* a long way off qualifying for one of the school rugby teams. It was a pretty miserable time. My mother and father tried their best to cheer me up. By that time my father had started up a youth team for Trimsaran RFC and he used to say it wouldn't be long before I was playing for them. By the time I did, of course, he was dead.

If he didn't see me progress beyond my early teens, Dad at least saw me play in a red shirt at the National Stadium in Cardiff. I was 11 at the time, playing for West Wales against East Wales in an Under-12s curtain-raiser to the Wales *v.* Tonga International in 1974. A couple of other future internationals, Adrian Hadley and Mark Ring, were on the opposite side.

Whether my father saw a future international in me that day is hard to say. He and my mother were given seats right at the back of the massive new stand from where, my mother recalls, I looked like a red-shirted ant.

But that little foretaste of the big time was before my move to Gwendraeth where for the first couple of years the chances of rugby glory were few. It was at this low ebb of my growing up that the first of the family tragedies hit me.

Living next door to my grandparents obviously made me very close to them. My grandfather was very strict with me and for a long time I thought he favoured my cousins but my mother explained that he didn't see them very often so he made a fuss of them when he did. He was more regularly involved with me and he took his grandfatherly duties seriously, forever lecturing me on the amount of time I spent on rugby instead of my schoolwork. Rugby will never get you anywhere, he used to say.

But I thought very highly of him and his death had a major impact on me. He was knocked down by a motor car one night and it was typical of him that, as he lay badly injured, he apologised to the driver of the car. Anyone else would have ranted and raved and at least thought about the insurance money. He took it all with great dignity and eventually died of the injuries he received. I was 12 years of age and, what with having to go to Gwendraeth, my world was starting to fall apart.

It seems sacrilege to mention the death of a dog when recalling a time of tragedy, but when my dog Ben, a cross between a Labrador and a Collie, died soon afterwards it was all the confirmation I needed to convince me that life was being pretty nasty.

But life was merely preparing me for what was to come and the first sign of that quickly followed the loss of my grandfather and my dog. At first my father just seemed to be suffering from yellow jaundice but he soon worsened and had to be admitted to Llanelli Hospital. It was diagnosed as cancer of the liver and his only hope was to be transferred to the famous Addenbrooke's Hospital in Cambridge where they were beginning to attempt liver transplants.

My mother was put under no illusions as to the seriousness of the situation and she made no attempt to hide it from me although Caroline was kept in the dark as much as possible. It was an appalling time for my mother who came to look very ill. From Trimsaran to Cambridge by public transport is a very difficult journey and once there she stayed in a bed-sitter, spending as much time as possible at the hospital. We couldn't have had a more brilliant surgeon than Professor Roy Calne's but the risks were still very high.

Dad was to be the first Welshman to have a liver transplant and only the third in Britain. Mammy took me up with her just before the operation and when I left his bedside to wait outside for her, I thought I would never see him again. I went into the hospital chapel and I really prayed. I'd pretended to pray many times in Sunday school but now, at just turned 13, I was praying hard for the first time in my life.

Professor Calne's operation was a great success and my father became a bit of a celebrity again. He was even introduced to Princess Margaret as one of their successes when she visited the liver unit at Cambridge.

He still needed lots of treatment, which entailed two visits to Carmarthen and one to Cambridge every week, so the strain on my mother was considerable. But at least we had him back and we even made it to the beach at Tenby that summer where we played bowls together with that same competitive edge.

But it was too good to last. Although the transplant had been a success, cancer was present elsewhere in his body including his stomach. So it was back to Cambridge where he had more severe surgery. He'd still want to know everything about my rugby when Mammy took me up there but it was clear that he was fighting a losing battle. One day I heard my mother explaining to Caroline that he was never going to get better and I broke down.

When they could do nothing more for him, he came home. One day the deputy headmaster came into the classroom and asked for me. I had been playing football in the break and I hit Alun Griffiths in the ear with the ball. He was crying and said he'd gone deaf. So, at first, I thought I was being called out to get punished. But suddenly I had a strange feeling. Before he said anything, I said, 'My father's dead, isn't he?'

When I reached home my mother was in the passage. I walked straight upstairs to see him. He had wanted two things in life – to see me play for Wales and to give Caroline away. He was to do neither. That evening, when the house was full of friends and relatives, I went down to the Welfare Hall to play pool and table tennis. I made early use of the village therapy.

There was more to come. During my father's year-long illness, many people offered help. The rugby club held a Past *v*. Present game and gave the proceeds to help my mother pay the fares to Cambridge. After his funeral, which was exactly a week before Christmas, a neighbour asked Mammy what arrangements she had made for Christmas. She replied that we wouldn't be bothering with Christmas. The neighbours were not too impressed with this attitude and she was practically frogmarched down to the shops and assisted to buy a couple of presents for me and Caroline and the basic festive things. It was obviously a quiet day for us but the neighbours had forced us to make the effort.

Mammy will not thank me for going on about how much I admire her but she stood up remarkably to the strain of that year, to watching Dad slowly die while tackling that terrible journey and worrying about her children. She lost so much weight but none of her courage. Even when it was all over and she was working in the school canteen nothing seemed to go smoothly.

When Dad was alive we used to go everywhere in the family car, a navy blue Morris 1000 whose number TTH 372D I will never forget. But Mammy couldn't drive and, apart from the practical advantages of having a car in an out-of-the-way place, Caroline and I missed our little outings. So Mammy took up driving lessons. But twice she took the test and twice she had to come home to tell us she'd failed. I don't think we were very patient with her. I now apologise.

She eventually passed at the third attempt (as I did) and life returned to a more convenient state. It must have been a struggle for her financially but we never seemed to go without the essentials.

When I first started to receive offers from rugby league clubs Mammy recalled that my father once had an offer to go north. It was in 1958, not long after they met. She was 18 and he was 25. The offer was from Leigh and was for £2000. My father had been brought up by his grandmother and she was then in need of looking after so he turned it down.

Dad's fellow centre at Swansea then was Gordon Lewis and a similar offer was put to him. Gordon, who came from Kidwelly, accepted and went on to make 379 appearances for Leigh and score 336 points. He thought my father was a very good player but he didn't know how he would have coped with league. Gordon was altogether bigger and yet he ended up in hospital twice in his first three games.

The point is that Gordon is still living in Leigh, and very happily so. Had my father gone I would have been born up there and likely still to be there. The good people of Leigh will have to forgive me when I say I'm glad my father stayed home.

Look at Emlyn Hughes. His father was a Llanelli player who went north and stayed there and Emlyn ended up as captain of the England soccer team – which shows the nasty things that can happen to you.

Actually, if my son Scott finishes up as a soccer international, I would be delighted. Only I'd have to insist he played for Wales.

He may well be brought up in Trimsaran because, before I moved to Widnes, I was already building a house in the village. Perhaps the following story illustrates my relationship with the place. I wanted to buy a plot of land which is adjacent to the clubhouse, from the rugby club, for £5000. They wanted £7000. So I jokingly said, I would take back the set of international jerseys I had donated to the club and sell them for £2000 to make up the difference. In the end they agreed to take £5000.

The story was told in a magazine article about me and I received a shirty letter from Trimsaran RFC asking me to appear before the committee and explain why I had revealed private club business. It mattered not to them who I was, or thought I was. I wasn't able to go before the committee but I wrote a letter of explanation and begged their forgiveness. I should have known better than to treat them lightly.

And that's how the relationship is. Any son of Trimsaran who figures he's made it big in the outside world had better leave his ego behind when he goes home to visit. They take a pride in your achievement and want to hear all about your adventures but they aren't impressed with self-importance.

It's a fair exchange, really. You bring credit to the village and they'll help you keep your feet on the ground. No matter how high you climb or how far you fall, they'll treat you just the same. High fliers couldn't ask for a more secure safety net.

3
Small Beginnings

Lightning never strikes twice in the same place, but in Wales lightning certainly comes from the same place. Electric outside halves like Barry John, Phil Bennett, Gareth Davies, Carwyn James and Gary Pearce have been bringing blinding flashes to rugby for the past 25 years and they all come from the same patch of largely rural land running up west from Llanelli towards Carmarthen.

A blanket ten miles square would cover this fertile area and near the heart of it is Trimsaran. Yet it was a long time before Jonathan Davies was hailed as worthy enough to be included in the illustrious company in whose shadows he grew up.

Considering the sacred role the fly-half occupies in Welsh sporting folklore, you would have thought that three wise men would have been on permanent standby to investigate any beckoning light in the sky. But Jonathan's potential managed to escape the attention of most of the prophets as he urged his diminutive frame into the schoolboy frays of West Wales.

There were one or two honourable exceptions, such as Carwyn James and Meirion Davies. Carwyn, the legendary Llanelli and British Lions coach, was very encouraging to the nine-year-old Davies, while from the day that Meirion, the former London Welsh, Cardiff and Llanelli hooker, walked into Trimsaran Primary school Jonathan's future was in steady hands.

But the majority saw just a skinny little kid, clever perhaps but, even by the undemanding standards of physique the game applies to half-backs, he was regrettably under-sized.

Here we touch upon the great paradox of rugby; in a game founded on attrition, on strength, power, height and robust athleticism, chief among its heroes is so often the weakest looking, most vulnerable player.

Very often the scrum-half will be the smallest in the team but they are traditionally tough with it. Garden gnomes are usually softer to the touch than scrum-halves, who exude a similar sort of pugnacity that causes an Alsatian to tiptoe past a Corgi. It is the man next to him – the outside half, fly half, stand-off, whichever name you choose to call him by – who normally has the flimsiest figure, the one who looks as if survival ought to be his first priority. Yet his is the most influential of positions. The way his artistry and creative powers can govern the game saves it from philistinism and allows us all to find a moral amid its fury.

If it is true that sport mirrors life then the rugby outside half, particularly one like Jonathan Davies, fulfils a major role. He is the official representative of the weak in the world of the mighty, the patron saint of the puny.

He is the living, glorious example that the battle is not always to the strong and powerful, that God can invest enough of his magic in one frail body to defeat all the forces of evil.

It is no surprise that the Welsh take this imagery further than most. Apart from a pressing need to beat the English regularly and the All Blacks occasionally, the Welsh are conscious of their reputation for culture. They enjoy the macho image represented by the rugged coalminer but no race will hush quicker at the first pluck of a harp-string or the clearing of a tenor's throat.

And no sporting audience appreciates more the touch of skill that suddenly elevates an afternoon of sweat, strain and strife. The great outside half is their Messiah and the nation is fortunate to have produced so many.

But few of them started out as small, had to fight as hard or wait as long for recognition as Jonathan. Not for him the triumphant procession up through the Welsh schoolboy teams which is the customary thoroughfare to the coveted No. 10 red jersey. His lack of schoolboy honours is surprising, but he may have contributed to this by an incident involving Trimsaran Youth which we will discuss later.

Carwyn James would have certainly been surprised, because he had no doubts about the boy's future. He first saw Jonathan play in an Under-11 seven-a-side tournament in which he had to choose the player of the tournament and present the trophy. Jonathan was only nine years old and up against boys two years older and much bigger but he was so outstanding that Carwyn had no hesitation in selecting him for the award. Not only that, he asked the organisers if Jonathan could keep the trophy instead of handing it back the following year. 'Don't worry,' Carwyn assured them, 'I'll buy a new trophy to replace it.'

Two years later, when Jonathan was 11, they met again. Carwyn had seen him play once or twice since and was delighted with his progress. He told Jonathan he was going to write a book on outside halves and he was including a chapter on internationals for the future. He said that Jonathan was going to play for Wales and that he was in line behind a 16-year-old whose name Jonathan cannot remember and Gareth Davies, who was a little older again. It was typical of Carwyn that he should have worked out the succession to the throne.

Alas, Carwyn died before Jonathan had a chance to prove his prediction right. The second player he mentioned did not make the senior Welsh team but the visionary at least scored two out of three – although he might have despaired of Jonathan fighting his way out of the doldrums that beset his teens.

Because of the Welsh Rugby Union's neglect in not appointing Carwyn to an influential position the great man was lost to Welsh rugby even before his untimely death. The effect of that loss may rumble on for years. Jonathan would have undoubtedly benefited from his counsel and encouragement.

That would have been a bonus on top of the massive contribution Jonathan received to his rugby development from Meirion Davies, who played under Carwyn's coaching at Llanelli and who also saw the potential in the pitifully small boy. Meirion was a Trimsaran boy, born in a farm on the outskirts of the village. When he qualified as a teacher he did what so many Welshmen did, he went to London to teach and play rugby. He played for London Welsh when they were becoming the country's leading club. He moved back to Wales to teach at Cardiff's Fitzalan High School and had four seasons with the Arms Park Club. Then he decided to move into the Primary sector, take a post at Trimsaran school and play for Llanelli.

As an old friend of Len Davies he was aware of Jonathan but it wasn't until he set about organising a school rugby team that he realised what an exceptional talent he was.

Meirion remembers, 'Although he was very, very small he was outstanding from the beginning. It was sheer talent with a ball that marked him out – and that was with any type of ball. All the good outside halves in Welsh rugby would have made excellent soccer players, Barry John and Phil Bennett especially, and Jonathan would have been the same. But he was totally committed to rugby. I don't remember seeing him without a rugby ball under his arm and he mastered the skills at a very early age.'

Meirion, who is now headmaster at Llanelli's Dewi Sant school, modestly deflects any credit for Jonathan's development. 'He was so naturally gifted he would have made it whatever the circumstances.'

Jonathan was 19 before he stepped into first class rugby and it is fair to question if that vital translation of raw genius into the practical language of the top level would have been completed at all without the basic grounding with which Meirion Davies began to fashion the wild and untamed talents of Trimsaran into a school team the village could be proud of.

Less sensitive coaches, and there appear to have been plenty of those around, might have been persuaded by the meagreness of Jonathan's physique to suggest less threatening pursuits. Even Llanelli, the team of his dreams, were later to turn him down out of hand because of his size.

His stepfather Ken recalls watching Jonathan play his first games before he was nine. 'He was all nose and hair – there was not much else you could see. But when he got the ball you'd forget about his size.'

Meirion was determined that his boys would learn rugby as a handling game. 'I encouraged them to run and pass the ball as much as possible. Kicking was an option when all else failed, and only then. Jonathan responded magnificently. He was two years younger than most of those around him and yet his was the mature mind, always willing to try things. He had such a lot of confidence and when he got into the big time he was still trying out the unexpected moves just as he did as a kid.

'I once saw him attempt to kick the ball downfield, miss the ball deliberately, catch it and run through the astonished opposition to score. I was looking forward to seeing him do that against England! It was that ability to do something from nothing that marked him out from the start. It is what Wales have missed most since he changed codes. He has that quality of doing the unexpected and the worse the service the more adventurous he becomes. He can turn bad balls to his advantage.'

Whenever Jonathan's size came up, Meirion would reason with him that lots of schoolboy rugby players excel because they are bigger and stronger than their contemporaries. Once the size difference was eliminated so was the superiority. But Jonathan was a good player without the size, he still had that to come.

'But he didn't develop physically until quite late. He must have been 17 or 18 before he began to grow substantially. He is not big now but he was late even getting to that stage. There was no doubt his size held him back, not in development but in people's acceptance of him.

'And it was unfair because he was always a keen tackler, very anxious to do his bit for the team. He wasn't able to meet them head-on all the time but he would get them down one way or another. It was never a problem with him. It was as if he had to prove that his size was not a handicap, and neither was it. He does more tackling than any outside half of recent memory other than David Watkins.'

Although Jonathan was not an enthusiastic scholar it was because of his preoccupation with rugby that he passed his 11-plus. As the exam loomed, Meirion put his foot down – no studying, no rugby. If the homework wasn't up to scratch the miscreant wouldn't be in the team. Jonathan didn't miss a match, and passed.

Winning a place at Gwendraeth Grammar was a mixed blessing for Jonathan. It was a fine school with an excellent tradition for producing great rugby stars but it separated him from his friends and pitched him into a world in which he would have to prove all over again that his size was no barrier to him playing excellent rugby.

It was to prove a rough ride even when he managed to fight his way into the school teams. Gwendraeth were by no means a big school numerically and he and his team-mates constantly found themselves up against bigger and better rivals. Skills, even those as promising and precocious as Jonathan's, need a proper platform. He had one in the strong Trimsaran team but now every game seemed a struggle against the odds. It may have been good for building character and courage but it was not an encouraging time.

He was 17 before the prospects of a Welsh schools cap loomed as a distinct possibility. But those prospects were wrecked when he fell foul of officialdom and he left Gwendraeth under a cloud.

He was half-way through an admittedly plaintive attempt at passing his A-levels when he decided to quit and take up an apprenticeship as a painter and decorator.

It was not a decision based on any impatience with education although he was far from being an enthusiastic scholar, but as a result of his first brush with Welsh rugby authorities. The brush cost him his last chance of a schools cap and led even to his beloved Trimsaran Youth being suspended.

▽ J.D.

It was the most exciting letter I had ever opened. It was April 1980 and I was 17 and despairing of ever getting near a Welsh cap. I had been told I was too small so often it was firmly embedded in my mind as a fact of life, even though I was starting to fill out.

But, suddenly, there was this letter from the Welsh Schools Rugby Union (Senior Group) inviting me to attend the selected course for potential international players at Aberystwyth from 26 July to 2 August. It was the customary get-together of players they considered likely to be challenging strongly for places in the Welsh senior schools team the following season. I had made the breakthrough after what had been a good season for me. I was in the East Dyfed Under-17 county team as well as the Gwendraeth School team and was playing for Trimsaran Youth whenever they didn't clash with a schools fixture, which had to have priority.

At the time I received the invitation I had been ill and off school. I'd had a garbled message via a friend about playing for East Dyfed against Mid Glamorgan in the semi-final of the Welsh County competition. Since I didn't know if I'd be well enough to play I did nothing about it.

Then came an SOS from Trimsaran Youth. They were playing in a Llanelli & District Cup final and had suffered a couple of injuries and were literally down to 14 men – could I play?

It was a terrible quandary because the Trimsaran game was on the same evening as the East Dyfed match. Mammy and I talked about it for hours. The games were the next day and although I felt well enough to play, who should it be for?

There was no doubt where my allegiance lay. Many of my boyhood pals were playing for Trimsaran Youth, which was the team my father founded with Ray James and Haydn Ford on behalf of Trimsaran RFC. And it was Trimsaran who raised the money to help my mother visit my father so often when he was in hospital in Cambridge. And I hadn't heard officially that I was wanted by East Dyfed. As far as the school was concerned I was still ill. . . .

It was a problem to know what to do for the best but, in the end, how could I turn down Trimsaran? So I played and after all that Trimsaran lost.

Two days later Mammy received a letter that tore my expectations apart. It was from Alan Lewis, the PE master at Gwendraeth. It read:

'I was extremely disappointed to learn that Jonathan had played on Tuesday for Trimsaran Youth. He had previously been selected to represent East Dyfed on the same evening and obviously the first loyalty of all pupils is to school rugby. Furthermore, had the proper procedure been adhered to, Trimsaran RFC should have sought my written permission to play any Gwendraeth Grammar School boy.

'Consequently, I have contacted Mr J. E. Williams, WSSRU coach, concerning the matter and it has been decided that Jonathan will not now be able to attend the selected course at Aberystwyth and another outside half will be found to take his place.'

The following day I received a letter from Mr Williams speaking of his 'extreme disappointment' and 'a serious breach of the rules' and confirming that 'although originally selected for the course at Aberystwyth, your name has now been withdrawn'.

The dejection in our house hardly needs describing. We realised that it was no use appealing but my mother was determined not to let it rest there.

She wrote back to Mr Williams: 'I would like to put right one remark made about Jonathan being disloyal to the school. Jonathan has played rugby for Gwendraeth Grammar School for the last five and a half years, two of those years being very difficult for us all because my husband died leaving us a little hard up.

'Jonathan was offered a weekend job which would have brought in about £15–£20 but we had a little conference and decided that he should be free to play rugby for the school on Saturday. Many boys from the village and Gwendraeth did take jobs but we thought his first concern should be to the school. I now realise that it was a very wrong decision. I hope this letter will help your committee to see that Jonathan is not a disloyal boy and that his only weakness is that his heart is too big and he tries to please everyone. I hope that if he does manage to go further in his rugby career that this one mistake will not be held against him.' Her plea was to no avail.

It was not long before my mother was taking up the pen again. This time in defence of Trimsaran RFC who had been reported to the Welsh Rugby Union over the incident. She related the full story. That I had been ill and away from school at the time. That I had been informed of the East Dyfed game only unofficially, by a garbled message via a friend and she had contributed to my decision by reminding me that we owed a debt of gratitude to the club because of my father. She even offered to attend a personal hearing.

It was to no avail. Trimsaran Youth were banned from playing rugby for the first month of the following season.

My mother had worked so hard to reduce the effect of losing a father on me and Caroline and she fought harder than ever to prevent this setback to my rugby career. I was more annoyed on her behalf than mine but it didn't help to convince me that fate was working in my favour.

A couple of years later, Alan Lewis, the PE teacher at Gwendraeth, called at the house. He was by then coach of Pontadulais who play in the West Wales League, and he was hoping I would sign for them. I was out at the time and Ken sent him away with a flea in his ear.

But Alan and I are good friends, despite what happened. He did a lot for me while I was at Gwendraeth and obviously felt very strongly about rugby at the school. What I did was against the rules but I feel he reacted a little hastily and might well have regretted the outcome. In fact I think we both regret it and we both would act differently if we faced that event again.

Even now when I look back on it the punishment seems savage. It wasn't a straightforward case of ignoring the school, who hadn't made much of an attempt to contact me to discover if I was well, and I was entitled to deeper than usual feelings about Trimsaran. To effectively bar me from playing for Welsh schools for an entire season, and that meant for ever, was a sentence I would have expected had I burned the school down!

I decided almost immediately to leave. My relationship with Alan was obviously strained and with my chances of representing Wales in my final year wiped out, there didn't seem much point in staying on. I'd had a good time and made good friends like Simon King, Aled Owen and the Trimsaran clique, but my A-level studies were not progressing all that favourably and I felt justified in bringing my scholastic career to an unhappy end.

I hadn't done all that well in my O-levels – I passed in Welsh and Geography and that was it – and had stayed on at school because Mammy wanted me to have every chance of getting as much education as I could. But all I really enjoyed was being in the gym at every opportunity and playing games. Although things have turned

41

out well I still regret not studying much harder, a mistake my son Scott won't make.

Had my father lived I think I would have achieved much more at school. It wasn't that my mother allowed me to neglect my work. She was forever badgering me about it but there is a limit to the amount of control a mother can have with a job, a house and two children to look after.

When I was attempting to do my homework I could hear a ball bounce 100 yards away, and I would be off in search of it. The presence of my father would have been likely to stop that. He would have added firmness to my mother's desire to see me well educated just as he did when I started playing rugby. My boots had to be clean, without a speck of the previous game's mud, my shirt, shorts and socks had to be clean and my socks held up neatly with an elastic band. Playing rugby was something special in his opinion and you had to be properly dressed for it.

I don't think I'm the dunce my exam results made me look and with a bit of application I might have even gone to university. I'm often asked if I regret that, because those lucky enough to play rugby at university, and especially at Oxford and Cambridge, seem to have a great life until their mid 20s and always seem to end up with good jobs.

Sometimes I do regret it, but I don't feel in any way hard done by. For a start, my enforced exit from school threw me into a much harder rugby environment. I learned more about the game and myself in the following two years than I could have possibly done had I stayed in the education stream.

To be truthful, school rugby had not been a great help in my development as a player. Trimsaran had been a great start for me because we had a very good team and I felt comfortable and confident. I had achieved recognition by being selected for Llanelli Under-11s and by starring in a number of seven-a-side tournaments. Even the great Carwyn James had paid me a compliment and predicted an international future.

But when I went to Gwendraeth I went to a school that had a splendid tradition for producing stars but, at the time I was there, was heavily outnumbered by surrounding schools.

There were 600 pupils at Gwendraeth, less than half the number of some of the giant comprehensives we had to meet on the rugby field. That couldn't be helped but it seemed that every time we took the field, we were up against bigger and better teams. It is not easy for individual players to shine when the side is not seeing much of the ball and getting a battering in the process.

Amman Valley Comprehensive, Llanelli GS, Gowerton GS – they were all tough battles and we always seemed to be battling against superior forces. And when I was picked for district matches it was not much easier. Our district was called Mynydd Mawr which did not have a big catchment area, so when we played Cardiff district, or Swansea, or Bridgend, the difference between the packs alone would mean a very slim ration of the ball for us.

The combination of being small and not getting the ball prevented me from making a big impression. But there was something else that was difficult to live with – the ghosts of the past.

It is very nice to come from an area renowned for producing great players but it has its disadvantages. Look at the outside halves who went to Gwendraeth. People would see me and say 'He's no Barry John,' or 'He'll never make a Gareth Davies'.

But at least you had something to aim at. I never saw Barry John play but I was one of the small boys at Stradey who used to idolise Phil Bennett. My father used to take me over to Stradey in the Morris Minor and I would sit transfixed.

I was there one Boxing Day when Llanelli played London Welsh. There were more stars on the pitch that day than there are in all Great Britain now. London Welsh were in their heyday with players like JPR, Gerald Davies, John Dawes, Mervyn Davies and John Taylor. Apart from Phil Bennett, Llanelli had stars like Andy Hill, J. J. Williams, Derek Quinnell, Ray Gravell and Delme Thomas.

And I was there when Llanelli beat the 1973 All Blacks, although from where I was sitting near the touchline I couldn't see much of Roy Bergier's try.

There was no shortage of heroes, even nearer my own age. When I was eight I first encountered Gary Pearce who contributed so much to Hull's success last season. He once played for Laugharne Youth in the same seven-a-side tournament as me. He must have been all of ten and he was brilliant. I followed his career very closely after that and little did I know when he left Llanelli to go north that I would follow him, first to Llanelli and then to rugby league.

But long before those momentous days, Llanelli were to deliver a blow that hit me with more force than a young man with my ambitions is prepared for. I was 18 and a year had passed since my bust up with the school had sent me out into the hard cruel world a little earlier than planned.

I didn't regard it as a calamity. School rugby had lost its appeal and since the classroom never had any appeal in the first place I was not a reluctant leaver, especially as my relationship with Karen which had made even school bearable was coming to a halt.

There was not a wide choice of careers and the family came to the quick and unanimous decision that I should follow my step-brother Peter in the painting and decorating trade. So I signed up for a three-year apprenticeship and settled down to a life of work and rugby that was thoroughly enjoyable.

I still had my ambitions. I still wanted to play for a first class club and for Wales, and although the rest of the world was proving slow to fit in with my dreams I don't recall any serious impatience.

It helped that I was back with my pals in Trimsaran Youth for whom I could now play without breaking any rules. There was the small matter of the month's ban we started the following season with, but that merely meant that most of us played in Trimsaran's second team.

So I found myself playing adult rugby in the sort of company that doesn't automatically welcome little whippersnappers, particularly cheeky ones. It certainly brought home the reality that I was out of schoolboy rugby now and standing shoulder to shoulder with men, only my shoulder was at least a foot lower than most of theirs.

Once Trimsaran Youth got under way again we began to have an excellent season, finishing by getting to the semi-final of the Welsh Youth Cup. What helped us tremendously was that Meirion Davies had by that time become coach to Trimsaran. So the principles he drilled into us at a very young age were reinforced at this later stage of our development.

At the end of that season, by which time I was 18, I felt sufficiently sure of myself to put my name forward for a trial with Llanelli. It was the summer of 1981 and when I was invited to play in a trial match at Stradey I could feel destiny calling.

I can't remember every detail about the game but I know I scored a try and that I finished pretty pleased with myself. I waited in vain after the match, like most of the young hopefuls that day I searched the faces of the Llanelli coaches for some sign of recognition. But for most of us it was a case of 'Don't ring us, we'll ring you'.

I got the impression that they thought I was a bit feeble. It was a reaction I was used to but that didn't ease the feeling of dejection. To have been rejected by the club I idolised, without the slightest word of encouragement or explanation, left me almost numb with disappointment.

What was worse was the feeling that followed. The realisation slowly dawned on me that I had fallen a long way behind my ambitions. Rugby is such an intense part of life in the area, that to have reached the age of 18 without some major recognition of your ability is to be virtually wiped out as a big-time prospect.

But although my self belief was lower than it has been before or since, I refused to accept that this was the end of my dreams. I didn't have much left to build a hope on. If I was going to make it I was the best kept secret in Wales, but there was still a spark left inside me.

It had always come down to my size. Right from when I was eight years old most people would not take me seriously as a rugby player until after they'd seen me play a few games. It still happens now. People in Widnes have stopped taking doubting looks at me but elsewhere when they watch me for the first time you can almost see the question mark forming in their minds.

And at 18 I was a lot less robust than I am now. My size has always prejudiced people against me and the fact I've had to battle all the harder to compensate for it has probably been a great advantage to me.

Certainly I needed no incentive to train harder than ever for the next rugby season. Meirion Davies had been his usual encouraging force, helping to convince me that a season in Trimsaran's first team in the hard West Wales scene would give me vital experience and a chance to show what I was really worth.

Trimsaran were playing just my type of rugby, a running game that enabled me to sharpen my handling skills against tough and competitive opponents and give me the chance to improvise and create.

Every moment that I wasn't wielding a paint brush I was training. I worked on my speed and strength and I could feel myself improving. I was playing in the sort of games in which tackles could not be shirked. I've always liked tackling and that season gave me every opportunity to sharpen up on techniques that sometimes required a strategically placed leg and a tug on a shirt.

What got through to me more than anything in the months following my rejection by Llanelli was that talent and skill on its own was not enough. You have to work and sweat to gain the strength you need to display your ability at its best. It was a lesson that stood me in good stead when I joined Widnes. The bigger the challenge the fitter you have to be.

The reward came unexpectedly. I was at the rugby club one Sunday evening watching television with the boys when someone opened the door of the lounge and shouted, 'Jonathan, you're wanted on the phone.'

'Who is it?' I shouted back, not wanting to take my eyes off whatever programme we were watching.

'David Shaw, fixtures secretary of Neath,' came the answer.

Every eye in the club watched me to the phone. When I finished talking and went into the bar, they said I'd gone a funny colour.

'They want me to play for Neath against Pontypridd on Tuesday,' I announced.

4

Triumph . . . and Disaster

If Wales could have raised armies as quickly as Trimsaran mobilises
a couple of coachloads to watch a son of the village perform on
some faraway field, the English invaders of centuries ago would
never have secured a footing.

It takes danger or disaster to motivate most communities but
Trimsaran rallies fastest when there's rugby duty to be done and
Jonathan has benefited richly by the parental pride the village has
displayed at every milestone of his progress.

No sooner had the word got out that he was to play for Neath,
the coach firm next door to the clubhouse was put on red alert to
ferry to Neath all those who had the evening off or could rapidly
bargain a swap in shifts. It was a journey of no more than 20 miles
but the movement there and back had to be planned, with a stop
en route and on return, and synchronised with those going by car.

Jonathan's stepfather Ken finished promptly at the end of his
morning shift as chargehand at the coal disposal plant and organised
the family car to include Jonathan, his mother, sister Caroline and
girlfriend Karen, who remembers Jonathan being grey with fear – a
colour she was not to see again until he played his first game for
Widnes.

Not only did Jonathan tremble uncontrollably all the way, they
had taken such sensible precautions against being late that the Gnoll
was deserted when they arrived.

Although it was a cold February day and no time to be hanging
about, that hour or so seemed nothing. The long wait for Jonathan
to receive just one chance to show what he could do at the top

level was almost over. Beneath the nervousness that Jonathan found impossible to disguise, he felt strangely confident. ·

Most people find it more convenient to be calm on the outside, and inwardly nervous. With Jonathan it was all arse backwards, as they say in Wales.

Neath committee man Ken Davies was the first person he saw that evening as he hovered self-consciously around the empty passages of the Gnoll, his neatly ironed kit burning a hole in his holdall.

Ken recalls wondering who the nervous little boy was. Then he discovered he was the latest in a long line of outside halves Neath had called up for trials in what was proving a very difficult season. Brian Thomas, the team manager who was to build Neath into arguably the best club in Britain, had yet to take office and a heavy defeat by Bridgend the previous Saturday had hung a black cloud over the club.

Jonathan Davies did not, at first sight, appear to be a player likely to fit it.

'I'd never seen him before. He'd been recommended to us as a promising little player but not only was he very nervous he looked as thin as a lath,' said Ken Davies.

There is often no finer hone to the edge of a boy's ambition than nervousness and Jonathan slowly calmed when he felt the outline of Neath's famous Maltese Cross emblem on the breast of his black shirt and he confidently sought the action in a close, hard-fought match.

He scored a try, cheekily dribbling the ball over the Pontypridd line before dropping hungrily upon it. And then, to clinch victory for Neath, he dropped a goal to make the score 19–13.

'He dropped the goal almost from the halfway line and for him to have played with such confidence and composure in what had been a struggling side brought us a great deal of pleasure and hope. We didn't realise it at the time but that game marked the turning point for Neath,' remembered Ken Davies, who was to become a close friend of Jonathan's.

Meanwhile the Trimsaran contingent headed for the bar with a double reason for celebration. Not only had Jonathan had a successful debut in his first major game, he had been selected for the Man of the Match award by former Wales and British Lions captain John Dawes. Although he had left before Jonathan emerged from the dressing room, Dawes chatted with Jonathan's family for a while and, when the conversation got around to other outside halves, said that he thought the next Welsh outside half was going to be Paul Turner.

His prediction was to take seven years to come true, during which time Jonathan filled the position 27 times before leaving it vacant for Turner when he moved up to Widnes early in 1989.

But the long occupation of the Welsh No. 10 shirt took a while to begin, even after that highly successful Neath debut. Although Jonathan was to play a few more matches for Neath that season, each outing confirming the promise of his debut, he was still registered as a Trimsaran player and he wanted to stay as one, partly because they were having a great season and partly because he had a good chance of playing for the Welsh District team and winning his first cap. Had he played five matches for Neath he would have been unable to see out the season with Trimsaran.

Having done that successfully he duly signed for Neath for the following season.

Ken Davies, being Welsh-speaking and friendly with Jonathan and his family, was deputed to visit Trimsaran one afternoon in June 1982 with the transfer forms. 'We were very worried that Swansea or Llanelli would step in first,' says Ken. 'After all, he was from their part of Wales and if we thought he was going to be great they must have had their eye on him, too. But there had been no approach from them and everyone agreed that he should join Neath and play for us in the big Snelling Sevens tournament that precedes the season.'

Once more the Trimsaran support group was mobilised, making for the National Stadium in Cardiff and a tournament which should have marked Jonathan's official arrival into top class rugby after many delays and disappointments. But he received an injury that was to inflict another 18 months of frustration on him – a further postponement of his progress that could so easily have been avoided with more prompt action and more influence in the right place.

Two years, almost to the day, elapsed between Jonathan's try-out for Neath and the re-start of his career with them. It was a comeback for someone who hadn't really been anywhere and came in a vital Cup match against Newport.

Ken Davies met Jonathan, 21 years old by now, before the match just as he had done two years previously.

'I am very keen on drop-goals and was always on to him to become an expert. That day I asked him to drop three goals, just for me. He dropped one and hit the post twice. He beat Newport on his own in that game and put himself and us back on the road to great things.'

▽ J.D.

When Neath gave me the trial that was eventually to prove the turning point of my life, I was the 13th outside half they had tried out that season. The figure didn't worry me because I was superstitious, which I am not, but because it gave the impression that either there were a lot of bad outside halves around or Neath were very, very fussy. Either way, it did my nerves no good at all.

I had been jittery since I answered the telephone in the Trimsaran clubhouse. I didn't believe it at first, thinking that the boys were playing a trick on me.

Oddly enough, I had been watching Neath play on television that afternoon. They had been hammered by Bridgend the previous day and Karen remembers me saying how awful it must be to play for a team as bad as that.

I probably told the boys the same thing so I was entitled to my suspicions. But it was confirmed in the paper next day. Bigger clubs frequently take players on permit from small clubs in order to have a look at them and I had received many offers from West Wales clubs which I turned down. But although Neath were not having a good season they were one of the great clubs. It was very much a dive in at the deep end but I sensed this was not only the biggest chance of my life but, if I messed it up, likely to be my last.

That realisation made me a nervous wreck long before we all piled into the family car for the journey to Neath. I was visibly shaking when we got there and we were so early, there wasn't a soul about.

The first person to come along was Ken Davies, the Neath committee man who was very helpful and kind to me and who has since become a close friend. He tried to put me at my ease and led me into the empty dressing room where I waited for the first Neath player to turn up. It happened to be Elgan Rees, the Welsh international winger and one of their best players, who was very friendly and encouraging. Grateful, I hung my clothes up on the peg next to his. I was to keep that same peg for the next four years, although I often felt it was a mistake.

Elgan, whose nickname is Harry, is a real gentleman and one of the best dressed people in the game. Naturally, being young and impressionable, I tried to emulate him. But no matter what I wore to games or training, Elgan made me feel as if I'd been kitted out by Oxfam.

But on that first night there was only one appearance I was worried about – the one I was about to make – and Elgan talked me through the waiting minutes, helping me to stay calm and concentrated. Ever since, I have made a point of introducing myself to new young players and trying to help them through what is a nerve-wracking experience.

It was a game I found a lot quicker than I was used to but I felt confident enough to follow my instincts. I scored a try and dropped a good goal towards the end and when I heard that John Dawes had given me the Man of the Match award there were not many happier young men in the country.

After that first match against Pontypridd, Neath wanted me to play more matches under permit but my first loyalty was to Trimsaran who were having a very good season. I was also in with a great chance of getting into the Welsh District team who were going to West Germany in the summer to play the Army. Had I played more than five games for Neath I would have been ineligible for the District team.

Trimsaran finished the season in fine style. We won our League, the Llanelli and District Cup and we reached the quarter finals of the Welsh Brewers' Cup.

Then came the news that I was in the District team. I was to wear the red shirt of Wales for the first time. Since it was also the first time I'd ever been abroad I was very excited.

But I'm afraid I faked my fitness. I had a very bad back that gave me a lot of pain but I told them I was fit. The prospect of being robbed of another chance of playing for Wales was too tempting. If I signed for Neath the following season I could never play for the Districts again. I'm glad to say that I managed to make my contribution and that we won. I got away with it but I've never felt right about it.

When I returned, Ken Davies turned up with the Neath transfer forms. Everyone in Trimsaran knew I had a decision to make and knew, too, that I didn't have much option. Ken was particularly anxious to get my signature as soon as possible because Neath thought that Llanelli were bound to be chasing me as well. But Llanelli had no such intentions and I happily agreed to join Neath, where I had the pleasure of being part of a club side that was to become the best in Britain.

My first appearance for Neath after signing was in their seven-a-side team in that great tournament, the Snelling Sevens, at Cardiff Arms Park. To my delight we were drawn in the same pool as Llanelli.

Exactly a year after I had played that unsuccessful trial match at Llanelli I was lining up against them in the colours of one of their deadliest rivals. I tried very hard to make them feel sorry but, although I scored a try, the final result was a 12–12 draw.

We both had to play Newbridge who were the third team in the pool and while we won our match, Llanelli didn't, so at least I had the satisfaction of helping their exit from the competition.

Neath went on to meet Abertillery in the quarter finals and we felt very confident about our chances of going all the way. We beat Abertillery but I didn't finish the game. Early in the second half, with no-one near me, I felt my knee ligaments go. It was ridiculously simple and yet it was obvious something serious had happened.

Had I gone straight to see a surgeon then, I would have been saved a lot of pain and trouble, and a year of my playing career.

But when I rested it seemed to get better so everyone was convinced it would mend itself. But every time I tried to play it would eventually start hurting so I would rest a couple of weeks and try again. This went on for ages until I played a match against Bedford. Everything was going fine until I took a pass and came off my right foot to beat a man. I felt it go with such a sickening feeling I knew I had a major injury.

But I still kept running and could hear the wing forward pounding after me. I put a grubber kick through with my good left foot and ran straight off the field. I'm not sure if the wing forward came after me but I did it all in one movement. It was pointless waiting for the trainer to come on the pitch. I knew my ligaments had gone.

After seeing so many physicians we decided to see a surgeon, Mr Maldwyn Griffith of Glangwili Hospital in Carmarthen. The first time we went Mammy and I waited four hours and didn't get to see him because he had an emergency.

We were luckier the next time, although I am not sure if lucky describes the news I heard after he'd examined the knee and found how badly torn the ligaments were. He said there was an operation known as the Macintosh Repair which was pretty complicated but if I didn't have it I would never play rugby again.

Before I could open my mouth Mammy said, 'Where do we sign?'

I've since become very good friends with Maldwyn and his secretary Nellie. They were so friendly and helpful – and brilliant too. The operation was a complete success and I have not had a twinge from that knee since. I managed to get Maldwyn tickets for a few internationals so he could watch his knee playing for Wales and I've tended to pop down to see him whenever I've had any injury problems. His opinion always gives me confidence.

I suppose, having so successfully recovered from a serious injury, I shouldn't complain. If it had been done any quicker perhaps it wouldn't have turned out so well. But there is no doubt that if I had seen Maldwyn earlier, the injury wouldn't have taken twice as much time as was necessary out of a vital stage of my career.

There were months wasted before I even knew how seriously the knee had been hurt. Had I been an established player with a big city club I would have probably got to a specialist much earlier. But in my ignorance I just kept hoping it would recover through rest.

My troubles weren't over even when Maldwyn had made his diagnosis and booked me for the operation. There was a long waiting list and the fact that I was a promising young rugby player who had played a few games for Neath cut no ice at all. I'm sure everyone on that list was just as important as me but my very life, my future depended on my getting back onto the rugby field.

I'd never heard of private medicine or had anyone who could pull a string for me. Every season you read of soccer and rugby players who injure their knees and are being operated upon within a day or two. They don't know how lucky they are. Rugby clubs should have a private scheme to ensure prompt treatment for serious injuries. They may not care to pay players but they ought to look after them when they are hurt. I would telephone a couple of times a week, pleading to be given some sort of priority. I told them that not being able to climb ladders to paint was putting my job under threat, which was true. Phil Bennett tried to push things through on my behalf, Brian Thomas even sent down an expensive bottle of malt whiskey – but nothing worked.

If the hospital had been in Neath or if I had been a known player, they might have taken pity. But it was April, eight months after I first hurt my knee, before I appeared under the big lights over Maldwyn's operating table.

There was still a long and painful way to go, even then.

I had discovered after my first game for Neath that it was Phil Bennett who first recommended me to them. Now my boyhood hero was to give me even greater help.

He had suffered a similar injury and knew what I was facing. 'As soon as you can work on the knee you've got to force yourself to build up its strength again and work on the wasted muscles. I used to cry my eyes out, it was so painful . . . but you have to battle your way through it,' he told me.

It was good advice and coming from where it did, had every chance of being followed to the letter.

Ken took two rails out of the landing bannisters so that I could sit on the landing and dangle my legs over the stairs. I put a weight on my foot and sat there for hours, straightening and bending the knee until I could bear it no more.

When I was able to run, I pounded up and down Trimsaran mountain. Then I gave the leg some extra work by loading a sock with sand and wrapping it around my ankle to make the running harder. Then someone in the village dug out an old army bandolier and loaded the pouches with iron filings. I looked even more odd on my daily runs around the village.

It broke my heart but gradually the knee became stronger and after four or five months I was able to resume light training with Neath. It was a long hard period of recovery and my reward came when I managed to get a game in the reserves. The boost I badly needed came very quickly in that game. I scored a try after 50 seconds and the knee stood up very well to all the pressure I put on it.

A few more of those, I thought, and I shall be asking for my place in the first team.

I didn't have to ask. They wanted to play me the very next game which could hardly have been tougher – the quarter final of the Welsh Cup against Newport.

I protested that I wasn't sure I was ready. That one reserve game in 18 months had hardly made me match fit. That I hadn't done enough kicking practice. That my ball handling would be rusty.

Brian Thomas was adamant that I was ready to return and Ron Waldron, the coach, put his hand on my shoulder and said, 'Jonathan, it's like farting. Once you've learned you never forget.'

It was a big shock and I felt really sorry for Ben Childs from Tenby who had been playing well at stand-off in my absence (ironically I later took his place in Llanelli's team but he is a forgiving man and we are still good friends).

Not for the first time, I ran out to play for Neath in a very nervous state.

The Trimsaran contingent were there in strength, probably sick of the sight of me running around the village with daft things around my ankle. I scored a drop goal and we won to go through to the semi-final. The knee stood up to the test and I was lucky enough to be named Man of the Match. I was back where I started from two years previously.

Since I only played for five years in first class rugby union, that time represented a sizeable proportion of my career. One discovery I made during that period of close medical examination was that I had a slight curvature of the spine and that one leg is half an inch shorter than the other. Perhaps that's my secret – I've got a built-in sidestep.

5

Life with the Bulldozers

Jonathan's instinct for taking the unexpected option is by no means confined to the rugby pitch where he has made the element of surprise one of the most potent skills at his disposal. He has in his nature an appetite for sudden change that explains much about a character so often misinterpreted in his short time in the public eye.

He has changed jobs, changed clubs and, most famously, changed games so abruptly that even those closest to him were startled. This shock comes partly because, paradoxically, he is a bit of a ditherer in his everyday life. He is not a patient young man and eventually loses patience even with his own dithering, whereupon he will act with a sudden decisiveness. He can sell dummies to his own family just as easily as he does to opponents.

His faith, his joy even, in his ability is a strength that saw him through the early years of his career when there wasn't much tangible proof of it. Those who see it as arrogance are making the usual misconception of a man who delights in his talent – especially one whose talent is so spontaneous it thrills him as much as it thrills the onlooker.

He will never blush himself to death but the truly arrogant will never admit him to their ranks. Yet he will quite happily agree with anyone who calls him arrogant, as if they are paying him a compliment. If he feels there is criticism implied in the description he has a stock answer – 'Only on the field and it's arrogance rather than ignorance' – which he tosses out nonchalantly.

But his friends and relatives see little evidence of an overbearing self-esteem. They will admit to a chirpy self-assurance – but would you send a creative artist out to face those brutes without even a little swagger of confidence to his step?

The boys he grew up with in Trimsaran recognise very few changes in him and would pounce unmercifully upon them if they did. He was always cheeky and irrepressible but he always had to make up with bravado what he lacked in bulk.

When they played against him in rugby they would forgive the mocking laugh as he sent them sprawling in the wrong direction because they knew it was more of a playful giggle than a taunt. Strangers would not take it so kindly and roll their sleeves higher for the next attempt to grab him.

Once he established that a roused temper was easier to confuse, Jonathan included in his repertoire one or two antics designed to raise the ire and lower the efficiency of the opposition.

It was a risky business but a rewarding one. Many a menacing wing forward, revelling in his job to spring from the scrum and clatter the outside half, would throw a practised snarl in the direction of his target only to find himself being blown a kiss or given a saucy wink. The resulting rush to get to grips with this cheeky little upstart often lost enough sense and calculation to make Jonathan's elusiveness easier.

He had practised these tricks at the highest level. John Jeffrey, the Scottish and British Lions wing forward, was once reduced to incoherent rage trying to catch up with the little Welshman and make him suffer for his cheek.

Peter Winterbottom, the great England wing forward, once complained to Jonathan over a drink after an international, 'It's my job to intimidate you, not the other way round.'

He has hesitated to use similar tactics in rugby league where the chances of the infuriated catching up with you are far greater than in union.

In his early pioneering and often painful days in league, he tended to adopt the old adage that a soft answer turneth away wrath, but he was soon searching for some extra dimension to the psychological warfare that is inevitably part of modern games.

His natural ebullience has another side effect – its capacity to make him the focal point for the more introverted. He matured early – his ration of immaturity was to catch up with him later – and he was inclined to lead rather than follow. This quality brought him the company, friendship and protection of bigger boys and at one time his mother was concerned that he was turning into a bit of a bully, a small-time gang boss, but the phase passed.

But he attracted friends easily and, displaying the hospitality bred into him by his family and his nationality, he was rarely without them. He would bring three or four home for lunch, tea or late night movie watching. His mother would get up in the morning never knowing how many boys she would find sleeping on the softer places around the house.

Precisely how mature he was did not dawn on her until her husband died. When Jonathan came home from school that day she expected that consoling a distraught 14-year-old would be another burden to bear but it was she who found consolation in his calmness and control.

'He was wonderful,' says his mother. 'Not only was he able to cope with his own feelings, he tried to help me cope with mine. Without being asked, it was Jonathan who took visitors into the front room to pay their last respects to Len. He saw it as his duty and I was proud of the way he did it.

'The funeral was a week before Christmas and I was dreading Christmas Day with just the four of us, my mother, Jonathan, Caroline and me. But he read that situation, too, and kept up a non-stop barrage of silly jokes that brought laughter to a home that badly needed it.'

It must be said at this point that Jonathan's jokes are an acquired taste. He has a boyish sense of humour and the worse the joke the more he enjoys telling it. A sample joke is: 'What did Humphrey Bogart and Orson Welles have in common? They both had beards, except Humphrey Bogart.'

His wife Karen was vaguely aware of him long before she became close to him or his humour. They won their places at Gwendraeth Grammar School in the same year and reported on the same day – Karen far more enthusiastically than Jonathan.

They were in the same form but while Karen was in the bilingual class Jonathan was in the Welsh class and her first recollection of him was when he was called up to the stage in morning assembly to receive some sort of rugby award. She only remembers that because he was scruffy, with no tie and a red windcheater.

While they were in their 12th and 13th years he occasionally attracted her attention but her impression was only of a boy constantly playing soccer or rugby and never without mud on his knees or the seat of his pants. He had the reputation for cheekiness but he shut up like a clam whenever girls were about.

He was 15 before his interest in her broke the dam of his shyness. It first manifested itself on a school trip to Italy and blossomed at the Form Five Christmas party. The relationship managed to survive an embarrassing experience at the school eisteddfod. Because they were of similarly small stature they were matched together as a pair in the folk dancing competition. Since he was captain of the school rugby team at that time, Jonathan's motivation for the dance fell somewhat short of wholehearted. His feet refused to twinkle like they do on the rugby pitch and every mistake was accompanied by grimaces and shrugs at the adjudicators who promptly flung him and the blushing Karen out of the competition.

But her parents liked him. He made his debut at their house in Cefneithin, which is about eight miles from Trimsaran and situated on the main Swansea–Carmarthen road, when he was 16 and sat silent and bashful while Karen's father Byron Hopkins congratulated him on rating front-parlour treatment with the best tablecloth and the bone china.

Byron was Director of Personnel and Management Services for Carmarthen County Council and suffered from kidney trouble. He had a successful transplant when Karen was 17 but at the time he first met Jonathan he had to spend hours every day on a dialysis machine that was installed at the back of the house. It was an unpleasant and tedious procedure but Karen and Jonathan would happily assist him and help pass the time away with him.

When Jonathan decided to leave school after his brush with the authorities, he abandoned his A-level studies to take up an apprenticeship as a painter. Karen, who had done well in her O-levels, remained to take her 'A's and the romance cooled until they were passing each other in the street without exchanging much more than a growl.

A few months later Jonathan played in a school Past *v.* Present game and scored a try from the halfway line that even Karen, who was no rugby enthusiast, had to applaud. It was a shy conquering hero who self-consciously approached her afterwards and the romance blossomed once more.

Her parents, Virene and Byron, were delighted to welcome Jonathan back into the fold. Alas, Karen made rather a mess of her A-levels, a failure not totally unconnected with her relationship with Jonathan. But she started work in the lab at Glangwili Hospital, obtained her ONC and HNC certificates and qualified as a medical technician. They became engaged when they were 19, in May 1982, by which time Karen was watching him play regularly and beginning to realise for the first time that he was an exceptional player.

'Having known Jonathan as a person long before I knew him as a rugby player I sometimes have trouble relating to his public image. Whatever impression he gives on the field he is certainly not arrogant off it. I don't think an arrogant person can ever get as nervous as he does. There are different degrees of nervousness – I'll never forget how grey he looked before he played his first game for Neath and he was even worse before his debut for Widnes – but he's not worth speaking to before any game, he gets so much on edge,' said Karen.

There was to be plenty of time off the edge soon after he and Karen got engaged. She was watching when he injured his knee in the Snelling Sevens and spent the next 18 months encouraging him through the long and tormented road back to fitness. 'For someone so sports minded to be denied the pleasure of playing anything for so long was a miserable experience for both of us,' she recalls.

At least they could plan ahead for their future, but even that was a difficult task. As he came to the end of his apprenticeship Jonathan realised that he would have to make way for another apprentice so he left to get a job with another painting firm. But although the money was better it still didn't seem enough to build a marriage on.

Then he saw an announcement that the opencast coalmine at Ffos Las, a few hundred yards from his home, had vacancies for labourers. The money was good, with plenty of overtime and Wimpeys the owners were promising security of employment for 25 years. Security is not a word often bandied about in places like Trimsaran. Jonathan volunteered immediately.

▽ J.D.

I often wonder what I would have become had I not been good at rugby. It is not easy to work out because if you are good at rugby, or think you are, it tends to become an obsession at an early age and blots out all other considerations.

It doesn't enter your head that it is not a professional game like soccer, that it is not necessarily the key to a comfortable living. All that matters is that you have promise and that is enough to tempt you to wrap your whole ambition around it.

It may well be a misguided view and that the wise move is to keep the game in perspective and make sure you get a good education and plan a secure career. That may be simple enough in communities where rugby doesn't rate such a high priority but where I come from rugby is a religion and to be gifted at it carries some sort of responsibility, like you've been called by the church to serve your fellow man. At least, that's how it seems.

But suppose I had been no good at it or just had enough skill to enjoy the game but not enough to give me any hope that I could play it at a high level. Rugby would then be part of my life but not the centre of it, and from an early age I would have been aware that I had to plan and work for some sort of future.

I don't think I'm dull. When I could be persuaded to put down the ball and concentrate on my schoolwork I did very well. There's every reason to think that if rugby hadn't distracted me I might be in a good, well-paid job. You might say that there's no reason why that shouldn't have happened anyhow, that I shouldn't have let rugby dominate my life in that way. That's easier said than done.

My father's death undoubtedly disrupted my life at a crucial time in my education. Because of our mutual love for rugby I was probably drawn even more towards the game, as if the closer I got to rugby the closer I would be to him. And, as I have explained earlier, the absence of his firm hand when I was going through those vital years between the ages of 14 and 16 affected me a great deal. My mother did her utmost to channel some of my interest into school but I took advantage of the situation and if you lose touch with schoolwork at that stage, you'll never catch up.

If all this sounds like I'm bemoaning my lot in life, let me hasten to add that I'm happy with the way things have turned out and I wouldn't exchange places with anyone, apart from the odd multi-millionaire. But I've had to go to great lengths to secure my future in rugby and I've been more fortunate than most players who have devoted their lives to rugby union.

It's all right if you come from the right background, have a family business to go into or get earmarked for one of the professions. You can enjoy and concentrate on your rugby at University, safe in the knowledge that the future is assured, that there is no financial penalty to be paid for your passion for the game and the time spent training and guesting for select sides.

But let's not forget the player who goes out to work at 16 and has to beg, borrow or steal time to train and play midweek. The more he gets on, the more demands the game will make on him and either his job or his game will suffer in the end.

This is the sort of player whose interests need looking after, whose plight needs to be understood more by the men who govern rugby. He is the man to whom it should not be illegal for a club to give a helping hand financially.

The high-flyers, those who get all the glory, are the ones who get fixed up with the easy jobs and can pick up the perks.

I've been on both sides of the fence and I know how difficult it is for the underprivileged players who occupy that vital level of rugby one rung below the top flight. You hear a lot about rugby using its income to foster the grass roots. A player with his face pressed into the mud might think he's nearer the grass roots than anyone is likely to get.

In the days before Neath gave me an unexpected chance, and I was coming to terms with an ambition that might not be fulfilled, I faced for the first time the serious question of what I was going to do with my life. I still had my dreams but they were a long way from coming true.

In the previous school holidays I had done a bit of 'hobbling' – the local name for moonlighting – with my brother Peter, helping out with the painting. It made sense that I should learn the trade and then I could go into business with him. So I got fixed up with an apprenticeship with Sellick at Pontyates. Most of the work was on new houses and so I began three years of climbing ladders to paint guttering, fascia boards and down-pipes – anything that wouldn't show up my slowly improving skills with the brush.

Since the whole point of an apprenticeship is to learn a trade that will, theoretically, keep you for the rest of your life you can't really complain about low wages or the jobs they give you. We had a day a week off to go to technical college in Cardigan, an hour's drive away, which helped to break the monotony.

For a large part of that three years I was suffering from my knee injury, and was off work altogether for 13 weeks, so I didn't even have my rugby to look forward to.

As my apprenticeship came to an end it was clear that there wasn't room for a fully trained painter so I anticipated the worst and left to get a job with another painter called Glyn Griffiths. I was bringing home £90 a week which was a big increase on my apprentice's pay but since Karen and I were saving to get married I was constantly on the lookout for better paid work.

Those who see my image as someone who puts money before all else will not be surprised that I became interested in a job at the Ffos Las opencast mine. The pay was £140 a week, but that wasn't the attraction – Wimpeys were guaranteeing 25 years' work at the mine. It is probably difficult for those who have never known insecurity to realise what a comfort the word security brings with it.

Anyhow, to the surprise of everyone I became a banksman at Ffos Las and part of my duties were to keep the fleet of bulldozers topped up with oil and water and clean the mud off them at the end of the day. The hours were terrible – 6 a.m. to 7 p.m. every weekday and 6 a.m. to 12 noon on Saturdays.

I didn't mind the work or the hours but after cleaning great lumps of mud from the front of a bulldozer I'd have to jump into Ken's car to go to Neath for training. I used to go into the club for a couple of pints of orange and fall asleep in the bar.

For three months I stuck it and then I had to tell Brian Thomas that the job was starting to affect my rugby. And I would have to stop playing because I couldn't give 100 per cent. Men who do that sort of job all their lives have my admiration.

Brian spoke to Neil O'Halloran, an industrialist friend of his, on my behalf and it was arranged that I was to have an interview with John Eventon at a painting and shot-blasting firm called John Wright (Blachwall) Ltd. By that time I had passed my driving test at the third attempt and had bought an old Morris Marina for £300 and so was able to relieve Ken of the years of ferrying me around. I drove down one evening after finishing the bulldozers to see John in Bonvilston. It was no pushover; I had to make the trip three times before I got the job.

The pay was about the same as I was getting from the opencast but there were fewer hours, there was a car provided and the job didn't have a bulldozer in sight. I was putting aside the overalls and becoming a white-collar worker. They say that Welsh rugby teams are not as tough as they were because so many players have forsaken manual work in favour of soft office jobs. I don't know if the theory is right but even if it is I don't think it should apply to outside halves.

My job, basically, was to tour the contracts we were undertaking in various parts of west Wales and to make sure our painters were happy and that the customers had no complaints. I would also help get new work and give John a hand with the estimating. It was a terrific job, meeting some great people and dealing with something I knew a bit about.

John Wright was part of Neil O'Halloran's group of companies and not only was it a very successful group it was also friendly and exciting. You couldn't find anyone more interested in sport than Neil. He was a sporting celebrity himself. A Cardiff boy, and a boilermaker by trade, he was a very good soccer player and it was no surprise when he was signed by Cardiff City who were then in the First Division. He made his first appearance against Charlton Athletic in December 1955 and made history by scoring three goals – the only player in Cardiff City's history to score a hat-trick in his debut.

Neil had that ability to make an impact on anything he decided to do and his football career was just part of an impressive climb from humble beginnings. He was to establish himself as a leading light in the Welsh industrial world and I am very grateful for the fact that he has never lost his passion for sport.

His first love, of course, was soccer. He became chairman of Barry Town and made it into one of Wales's most successful non-League clubs. But he also loved rugby and I hope he doesn't regret employing two rugby players to help his business.

The first was Terry Holmes, who gave marvellous service to Cardiff and Wales before turning to rugby league with Bradford Northern. Terry is also a Cardiff boy and was in the scrap metal business before he joined Neil's Erection and Welding Group as a director.

Terry is an extremely popular person and proved to be an asset to Neil's operation, not only because of his knowledge of the scene but because people were always delighted to meet and talk to him. He was already well established as a rugby star and one of Neil's executives before I arrived and there's no doubt that the success he made of the job persuaded Neil to take on another rugby man.

Apart from the fact I idolised him as a player, Terry was super to work with and I learned a lot from his relaxed and easy style with people. Obviously, the job suited me because I was able to find the time to train and travel. As long as I made up the time it was the perfect situation; a life balanced flexibly between work and rugby, and when you were concentrating on one you could forget about the other.

I am sure it helped me to become more secure and confident as I set about establishing myself in first class rugby. I hope Neil felt I kept up my part of the bargain. You hear of so many rugby players

Below: Master and pupil. Posing with my father as a three-year-old

Right: Proud mother and son the day after my first cap in 1985

Trimsaran RFC in the early sixties. My father Len is far left in the back row and Ken, who was to become my stepfather, is on the right of the middle row

With Karen and Scott in June 1989

Nine years old and in the victorious Trimsaran Primary School team in the Kidwelly Sevens, Under-11s. I'm on the left of the back row, next to Merion Davies, the teacher who guided me into organised rugby

Left: Captain of Neath, and politely discussing a decision with the ref in the Cup semi-final against Cardiff in 1987

Below: Passing to Llanelli team-mate and best friend Ieaun Evans to give him yet another easy try!

Left: Keeping Rob Andrew at arm's length in an England–Wales international

Right: Getting a pass away against the French in 1986, despite a big load on my mind

Below: Out of action after a cartilege operation at Llanelli

Playing for the Barbarians at Cardiff and another confrontation with my predecessor in the Gwendraeth, Llanelli and Welsh teams, Gareth Davies

Above: The great French full-back Serge Blanco goes one way and, gratefully, I go another
Below: Where it began – the Trimsaran pitch and the open-cast coalmine in the background

Above left: A Welsh
squad training
session. Robert Jones
(left) and Bleddyn
Bowen (right) join me
in a typically exciting
and demanding work-
out!

Below left: On my
way to a vital try
against Scotland in
our Triple Crown
season, 1987–88. I've
cut back inside Finlay
Calder (on ground)
and Andrew Ker and
I've kicked for the line

Above: My last try for
Wales – against
Western Samoa in
November 1988

Right: My last try for
Llanelli – against
Swansea on 2 January
1989. Bleddyn Bowen
(No. 10) tackled me
as I went over and
still swears it wasn't a
try

Still one of my proudest moments – being Captain of Wales. We line up for the camera before the ill-fated match against Romania in December 1988 – my last time as captain

Braced for a tackle on David Campese, supported by a few friends, when the Australians met the Barbarians at Cardiff in November 1988

who join firms to become no more than an ornament, a mascot to be trotted out to impress the customers. I think I made a far more significant contribution to the wellbeing of the business than that.

But, let's face it, both Terry and I were there because we were well known rugby players. That we earned our keep was down to Neil's ability to select players who knew a bit about the business they were coming into, but that doesn't alter the fact that we were earning a living largely because of our rugby reputations. We were not earning a fortune, certainly not as much as some get from jobs which cash in on their rugby stardom, but how is that not benefiting from the game?

Rugby union does not realise how much it owes to employers like Neil. The game's health, and wealth, depends on its top players achieving and maintaining a high standard of skill and fitness and yet the authorities do nothing to make it easier for them to do this.

I want to return to this whole subject at greater length later. The point I am making in this context is that rugby happily turns a blind eye to many activities that make its high moral amateur stance a nonsense. They are content to let the skill and generosity of men like Neil produce players who are fit, well-trained and secure – players from whom the game derives almost all the income that allows it to flourish and thrive, and its top administrators to travel the world in luxury.

And yet they will do nothing, make no effort, give no consideration to what they could do to ease the player's lot amid the increasing demands of the modern game.

The player either fends for himself, has the good luck to find a kind employer, or struggles to keep his place in an amateur game only professionals can succeed in.

I wondered at the beginning what I would have been had I not devoted myself to the worship of rugby at an early age. Trimsaran doesn't produce many brain surgeons but I may have discovered some talent that has so far remained hidden. Many men make sacrifices for rugby and not many are rewarded in the way I have been. I often look back and consider that if I hadn't been thought worthy of being rescued from scraping mud off bulldozer blades my reward would have been much different.

6
Acting on Instinct

Trying to get a great player to explain his talent is like asking a bird to tell you how it flies. The truth is that our sporting heroes usually don't know why they can perform sudden acts of brilliance any more than the rest of us know why we can't.

During the course of discovering what makes Jonathan Davies tick I several times flung the question at him unexpectedly, hoping to get an instinctive response that might have given a glimmer of understanding about the origin of his skill, but a shrug is all I got. The last time I tried we were on a golf course where he was displaying very welcome signs of ordinariness. 'Look,' he said exasperatedly, 'if I knew that I'd probably know how to hit this bloody golf ball straight.'

Obviously, the mechanism of a rugby maestro has to include the vital parts of speed, guile, vision, handling, passing and kicking – all in good working order and regularly serviced. But that's only the start of it. Jonathan would consider speed to be his most valuable asset because only pace can get you where you need to be.

But when and where to run, how to see the half-gaps even before they appear, is the mystic quality that puts him in the top handful of memorable outside halves and is enabling him to make rapid headway in picking up the intricacies of rugby league.

He learned that skill from no-one and will never be able to pass it on, except through his genes perhaps. But what he did need was the proper vehicle for his talent, a suitable team context in which he would have the space, the ball and the support to fulfil his potential.

Fate, and the eagle eye of a club desperate for that touch of class necessary for success among the rough and rugged rivalries of Welsh club rugby, took him to the Gnoll just at the time Neath were trying to get themselves out of a rare trip through the doldrums.

What Jonathan could contribute was amply demonstrated even in the handful of games he played before his costly injury, but that might not have been enough had the Neath club not undergone a fundamental change in organisation and approach.

The man who was to revitalise them was not even a club official when Jonathan made his debut in February 1982. He was at the game but only as a spectator. Brian Thomas had yet to be called upon to take charge and lead Neath to achievements that placed them among Britain's finest clubs.

Thomas was an outstanding second row forward in the 'sixties, playing for Cambridge, Neath and Wales, and had a reputation for a robust, uncompromising style that was carried over into his team management techniques. But he had an eye for skill and a willingness to see it expressed freely in his team. Once or twice he was to clash with Jonathan over certain tactical differences but there is no doubt that he created the launching pad not only for Neath's upward surge but also for Jonathan's rapid rise.

He had seen Jonathan play once before that first game against Pontypridd. 'I first saw him in a Welsh Youth trial game when he was overlooked in favour of someone else. But I had him chalked up in my mind straight away. He looked the part. His size didn't matter because he had that very slick, arrogant air about him. He wanted to take charge. Then I saw him again in that first match at the Gnoll and there it was again – the unmistakable look of a player who knows what he wants to do and does it. It was amazing that no-one else had picked him out.'

Thomas was made team manager of Neath that summer and immediately set about organising the club, delegating specific duties to his two coaches and captain, and creating a style of play based on fast, hard working, ball-winning forwards and a pair of superb half backs.

Jonathan's injury in the Snelling Sevens was an early setback to those plans. Thomas was not pleased. 'He has a passion for showing off that is well served by sevens rugby. It appeals to the extrovert in him. But a twisted knee trying something special cost him 18 months of his career.'

The impact Thomas was to have on Neath ensured that the club did not suffer as much frustration as Jonathan during that time.

They went to the Schweppes Cup Final in 1983 and began to take on the appearance of a progressive team and in Ben Childs they found an outside half well able to respond to the team's requirements.

But Thomas was aware that they needed that extra something that only one outside half in ten thousand could provide and he was convinced that Jonathan, despite his alarming lack of first class experience, was that player. It was Thomas who insisted that Jonathan should come back into the team after only one warm-up game in the reserves. He was sure the boy, by then 21 years of age, would not let him down, even in a quarter-final Cup tie against Newport. He was right. Jonathan shrugged off 18 months of rust and put on a display that the local newspaper saw fit to describe as 'an outstanding a performance as anyone can remember from a fly-half'. He scored 19 points, and Ken Davies recalls the thrill that ran through the whole club, not just at that particular performance but at what it promised for the future.

'If anyone doubted he was a natural, that game would have convinced them. He had been out of rugby for virtually 18 months and yet walked out to take control of the match like a veteran. Brian Thomas had already created a very good side, Jonathan was to be the icing on the cake,' said Ken.

Jonathan's capacity to make the most of situations that look unlikely to bring the best out of him has never been better proved than in debuts. His first appearances in seven-a-side tournament finals as a nine and ten year-old; his first game for Neath and his comeback two years later; his debut for Wales; his entry into world-class sevens; his debut for Llanelli and even in Rugby League for Widnes. Each match represented a major step-up in class or a completely new environment and were marked by at least a very good display and mostly by a brilliant one.

That the results have been as much a surprise and delight to him as to anyone else, reveals the extent to which his game revolves around pure instinct.

But it wasn't only this that has set him apart. Brian Thomas, one of the most jealous guardians of the team ethic, rates Jonathan the best outside half he has ever seen because he is the most complete.

'He is the top in my estimation because he was as effective in defence as he was in attack. You put speed, skill, guts and confidence together and you have a great player. But he had something else not normally found in that position. He was mean, sometimes even nasty. He may look vulnerable but he can be nasty when it comes to looking after himself, and that is a vital weapon to have when you are as good as he is. He'll most likely get his nose bent in league but they will find out that if they are unduly nasty to him, he is capable of being just as nasty to them.'

Since this was the first indication of a slight stain on our hero's image of innocent brilliance, it was worth mentioning to him. Another one of those shrugs prefaced the explanation: 'Don't forget I didn't spend much time in schools rugby. My apprenticeship was mainly in senior rugby in West Wales where you have to look after yourself and for it to be known that you can.'

Those who were with him in the Trimsaran team would not disagree. One of them played with Jonathan's father, Len, and was still in the team when Jonathan first appeared. 'I don't know where Jonathan gets his aggression from but it wasn't his father. Len was a terrific player but he didn't have a nasty bone in his body. Jonathan is different – he won't put up with any nonsense.'

Others who played with him tell of how retribution for brutal treatment at the hands, or feet, of a wing forward would be gained by Jonathan in such a subtle way that it would be noticed by no-one except the recipient. It is relatively easy for a player of impeccable timing to arrange a punt downfield so that the kicking boot has reached an inconvenient height just as an onrushing opponent reaches him.

Brian Thomas sees this aggressive spirit as an essential strength but there were times when it clashed with Brian's own qualities of that nature. It ensured that their relationship, which was very strong and mutually respectful, was not always smooth and sweet.

Their closeness was reflected when the club made Jonathan captain when he was 23, by which time Brian had acknowledged that there was little, if anything, that Jonathan needed to be guided upon when he went on the pitch. Not that it was easy to make him listen.

'The only thing you really had to try to harness was his kicking. He always wanted to keep the ball in play, when there were occasions when it would have paid to put the ball out of play. I never really persuaded him. There were times when he thought it necessary to put the ball into touch but he would much prefer to keep it alive, to put the full back under pressure and he had a knack of doing that which few others have.'

Cliff Morgan rated Jonathan's vision as one of his most outstanding talents – the ability to see or be aware of the whole pitch and the pattern of play developing and who was where and which opponent was straying out of position. 'It is a rare skill, one that helped Pele to be such a great soccer player. If you see exactly what's happening in the game and have the ability to act quickly and decisively, you have a major advantage. And Jonathan has always had that quality.'

It is this clarity of awareness, in comparison to the panic-inducing blur that besets ordinary players when they get possession, that gives the star player that vital extra second or so to cause his damage.

Jonathan even keeps an eye on the crowd. His former boss Neil O'Halloran tells the story of how Jonathan was retrieving the ball from the running track prior to taking a vital kick during an international against Scotland at the Arms Park. As he picked up the ball he looked into the sea of faces in the north stand and saw one of their customers a dozen rows back.

'Hey, Tom, how you doing,' he shouted, waving as if he'd spotted him across the street. Then he turned and whacked the ball over.

Said Neil, 'The customer couldn't believe he'd been recognised and acknowledged out of 60,000 people. I think we've got him for life.'

When Jonathan was playing for the Barbarians against Australia at the Arms Park in November 1988 I saw him waving at someone in the stand during the game. I asked him afterwards who he'd been waving at. 'You,' he said, 'You didn't wave back so I thought you hadn't seen me.'

I said that even had I known it was me he'd spotted, I doubted if the understanding of a rugby press box had reached the level which would tolerate one of its number waving at a player.

▽ J.D.

I've learned many things from many people but I've never learned anything about outside half play from anyone. I've had lots of advice, most of it well-meaning, but none of it has made any difference to the way I play. I just go out and do what I think is best for the team and what we are trying to achieve at any particular time.

If I was going to listen to anyone I would have listened to my father but I didn't have to. Although I didn't realise it at the time, he had the great wisdom to realise that advice is meaningless if you haven't the ability to put it into practice. And if you have got the ability, you don't need the advice.

His precious gift to me, apart from what he passed down through his blood, was to create a love of playing with a ball, any ball. Because of who he was it was inevitable that a rugby ball would figure largest in my life but he knew that the important thing was to bring out the natural feeling for a ball.

And when Meirion Davies first introduced me and my friends to organised rugby at Trimsaran Primary School he did no more than explain the rules and positions and discourage us from kicking. The rest was instinct and I think it is significant that many of the things I do now first came into my head when I was 11 or under.

I have approached every major stepping-stone in my career with the same attitude, with nothing in my head except anxiety about how I was going to fare. The more challenges I met and overcame, the more my confidence grew. I am still getting nervous because each game is still a step into the unknown. I am confident that I will be able to cope with anything the game demands of me, but I never know until it happens. Everyone should have nerves as part of the process of preparing for a big challenge.

If all this suggests that I owe nothing to anyone then I am insulting many people. Rugby is a team game; more than that, it is a club game. On and off the field there are so many minds and bodies involved that it is a nerve for a player to think of his efforts and achievements in a personal way. My only excuse is that an outside half does depend on being able to show some individual skills, if only to keep him out of the clutches of the predators who prowl both codes.

I can recall only once when my total reliance on instinct was directly challenged. It was by Brian Thomas, one of the most powerful influences in my rugby career.

We were in the dressing rooms at Bridgend who were a very good side at the time and were about to give us a hard game.

Brian said to me, 'Jonathan, whenever you get the ball I want you to bang it as far into touch as you can.'

I said, 'Sorry, Brian, I'll decide what to do when I get the ball. I'll play it as I see fit.'

'Never mind about that,' he shouted, 'I want it in touch.'

I took my shirt off and offered it to him. 'Do you want this?' I demanded.

'Do you want a broken nose?' he asked.

I put the shirt back on and, strangely enough, I did put in quite a few long touch-kicks in that game. But I did so because that's what my instinct told me to do at the time; the boys might have thought I was doing what I was told but Brian had predicted what our game would require – I didn't know until I got out there!

The point is that the downfall of many an outside half is not that they lack ability but that they get their heads so full of orders and advice and tactics that their natural instincts get pushed into the background. Every time they receive the ball they have to pause that vital split second before they decide what to do, and too often that hesitation is fatal.

I am sure that so many players in all forms of football, be it soccer or rugby, go wrong because they are asked to conform to a formula, a pre-set plan that removes all chance of acting on instinct. The result, again seen in all codes, is a boring and sterile game whose only object is to avoid defeat. I'd rather not play the game than be negative and I am certain that in the long run people will stop paying to watch negative play. It is possible for any game to develop a period of stalemate but as long as I know there are players out there who have the skill and freedom to trust to their instinct, I will wait patiently for that moment of magic that makes sport so worthwhile. And as long as I am playing I will want to try to aim for that moment when I can produce something special – for my own sake as well as everyone else's.

By telling that story about Brian Thomas I was merely showing that sometimes the needs of team and individual do clash. But Brian played a major part in my development purely because he was keen for me to express myself. His approach to the game was based on creating a framework in which players could display their talents. But winning is the most important object and the only time I will ever do anything purposely negative is to preserve a winning situation for my team.

Brian encouraged me to think for myself because he realised I wasn't very good at carrying out instructions. Many have talked about my speed off the mark but they neglect to take into consideration that the fastest thing off the mark is my brain. That's why I don't need it to be cluttered up with instructions.

My instinct decides the best option even as the ball is coming into my hands. I've gained a yard on the opposition before my feet have moved. Being positive about what I am going to do is the main fuel for my surges and it's amazing how much faster you can be if you know where you are going.

Sometimes I've set off even before I am sure myself where I am headed for. It is a most exciting feeling and I get as much thrill as the crowd do because often it is as much a surprise to me that I've found a gap as it is to them. And if I seem to be pleased about it, it's not arrogance but simply the pleasure I've experienced. After all, if the crowd can enjoy it why can't I?

This all explains, I hope, how it was that after 18 months' lay off with my knee injury I was able to come back and claim the Man of the Match award. I just went out and put my trust in my instinct.

Brian, if I remember rightly, did no more than murmur a few encouraging words and I went out to help to put us into the semi-final of the Schweppes Cup against Aberavon.

It was round about this time that I joined Neil O'Halloran's firm and to come into contact with two such strong and forceful characters as Brian and Neil was very good for a 21-year-old. I learned a great deal from both of them – how to conduct myself, have faith in myself, sum people up, sort out the goodies from the baddies. It was better than any university and I still feel myself obeying certain rules about dealing with people that they taught me.

Both at work and at rugby I was under the influence of men who knew what they were doing. When I think of other places I could have gone to and the people who might have controlled my life I thank God for my good fortune.

They might both have wished that I'd been a little less headstrong but they needn't have worried – there were other restraining forces at work.

One of the big differences about playing for Neath instead of Trimsaran was that most of the talking I did on the pitch, and I do tend to chatter on a bit, was in English. In Trimsaran Welsh was the first and, most of the time, the only language.

At the Gnoll, Elgan Rees spoke Welsh as did the farmers like Kevin Phillips, the hooker, and Brian Williams. But most of the conversation was in English, it being the case that the further east you go in South Wales the less Welsh is spoken.

When we played Aberavon in the semi-final we beat them and suddenly I realised we were in the final. I was going to be playing at the National Stadium at Cardiff Arms Park and I was even prouder when Welsh TV asked me to give them an interview. It was my first time on television and I preened myself as the interviewer asked me in perfect Welsh, 'Sut wyt ti'n teimlio?' (How do you feel?). I told him exactly how I felt. 'It's a dream come true.' I gasped. Then I stared at him in horror. I'd replied in English! Instead

73

of saying 'breuddwyd wedi dod yn wir' the excitement of the moment had turned my words.

This is not a story aimed at the English or their language. As I have explained, I was brought up in Welsh and in Trimsaran that is what we talk. If we are in the company of those who only speak English then we speak English. But it is our second language and still has the reputation of being the posh language.

For me to use English at a time like that was to exhibit airs and graces way above my station. When I got back to the club in Trimsaran that evening I was hoping no-one had seen the television. But as I walked through the door everyone started chanting 'Dream come true, dream come true . . . '. I still haven't lived it down, not in the village or with Welsh-speaking rugby players. It was not looked upon as the act of a humble man.

But, whatever the language, it *was* a dream come true. Because of Neath's squad system I did not play in every game between my comeback in February and the end of the season, so I doubt if I had played in more than a dozen first class matches before I played in the Cup Final.

The fact that we were meeting Cardiff in the final was an added bonus. My new working colleague Terry Holmes was one of their star players and as soon as we knew we were going to meet, the banter between us built up to a fever pitch. He must have thought I was a very cheeky young man, trying to intimidate someone who was already enshrined as one of the all-time Welsh giants.

But Cardiff had more to offer than just Terry. At outside half was another hero of mine, Gareth Davies, a former pupil at Gwendraeth and a star product of the outside half factory. There was also the great lock Bob Norster, John Scott the English captain and No. 8, Mark Ring, one of the great centres, and Adrian Hadley the Welsh international winger who was on the opposing side when I made my debut for Widnes against Salford.

They were probably the most formidable side in Britain at that time and as Neath were still in the process of being built up as a power by Brian Thomas, we were not given much of a chance. One extra treat for me was that another Trimsaran boy Carl Bridgewater had forced his way into the Neath team. There were barely enough coaches in Trimsaran to bring them all to the National Stadium.

I am afraid the occasion got the better of my senses. Probably trying to prove that I was not over-awed by playing opposite the reigning Welsh outside half, I rushed at Gareth as he was making a kick early in the game and hit him with a late tackle.

It said a lot for my power that he wasn't hurt a bit. As I trotted back to my position Terry Holmes said quietly, 'That's enough of that now Jon.'

I took his rebuke and, since the tackle was out of character anyway, didn't repeat it. Perhaps I was aware that the odds were heavily stacked against us. In the end we lost 26–19 and made a good game of it. I didn't have a great game but I was pleased enough with my performance considering who we were up against. This was the big time, and I had had a taste of it.

7

The Cap Fits

Few things are more agonising than a Welshman's wait for his first cap. Some 99.99 per cent see their names deleted from candidature at a brutally early age but that sharp cut is nothing compared to those who lose out much further along the line. Too many good players have battled their way to the brink of selection and have waited there in vain. Some even make it to the substitutes' bench and actually wear the red shirt, but never step out to get it aired by the massed hot breath of their countrymen. Ray Thomas, the Llanelli hooker, was substitute for 24 games and never played, not for a minute.

The time Jonathan spent on the threshold was mercifully brief. Although he was scarcely a teenaged wonder when he was first selected – he was 22 years and six months – his progress to the international arena was comparatively brisk.

If you take his February 1984 comeback to the Neath ranks as the real starting date of his first class career, he was chosen after only 14 months and about 35 games. And during that time he had quickly graduated through membership of the squad, a 'B' international and a place on the substitutes' bench.

But the circumstances of his call-up were unusual enough to make even his short wait extremely tense. He was probably fortunate that the first international of 1985, against England at Cardiff, was postponed because of bad weather and put back until 20 April. This meant that Wales's first match of the Five Nations Championship was played against Scotland at Murrayfield where Wales won 25–21. But the following match was in Cardiff where Wales lost 21–9 to the eventual champions, Ireland. Then came the trip to Paris to play France, where a 14–3 defeat cast a national gloom.

Who knows, had Wales played England when they should have, and had they won as they usually do, the resulting confidence might have carried them into a more successful Championship. As it was, by the time they came to the rearranged match against England there was little left to do but experiment and Gareth Davies, who had been recalled to the outside half berth three matches earlier, was made chief scapegoat. But even that was botched in a manner that has become a regrettable part of the Welsh rugby scene.

When the WRU named the team to play England, the name A. N. Other occupied the outside half position. The selectors announced that they wanted another look at the candidates before filling this most vital vacancy. To put Gareth Davies, holder of 21 caps and a former captain of Wales, on probation as it were, was a greatly demeaning act and, devastated, he took the only honourable course of action. He immediately announced his retirement from international rugby.

Naturally, the air was buzzing with conjecture. Would the selectors go for someone with international experience, like Malcolm Dacey, or for an untried player like Jonathan?

There was only one Saturday left before the selectors had to make up their minds and, ironically, Dacey was playing for Swansea against Gareth's Cardiff that day. Davies was given a great reception by the Arms Park crowd and he went out to give an outside half display that completely outclassed Dacey's offering.

Jonathan, meanwhile, was playing for Neath against Gloucester at the Gnoll and the Welsh coach John Bevan (later to succumb to a fatal illness) and a couple of selectors saw him play a typically audacious game. Despite playing into a strong wind in the first half, Jonathan's adventurous kicking earned Neath a half-time lead which he helped to preserve with a try-saving tackle in the second half.

There had been no indication when the selectors would make their decision but they didn't leave it long. Next morning Rod Morgan, chairman of selectors, rang. 'Congratulations Jonathan,' he said, 'you have been selected to play against England.'

Jonathan hesitated. He remembered that Rod had used exactly the same words a few weeks earlier when he rang to tell him he was substitute against France. 'As substitute?' he asked. 'No, outside half,' was the reply.

The Trimsaran Over-35 team had left early that Sunday morning to play in Gloucester and at 2.45 p.m. were comfortably ensconced in the clubhouse. Like most Over-35 teams they were made up mainly of men who were clinging to the rugby skills of their youth with as much success as they held on to their sobriety afterwards, and by that time of the afternoon the sing-song had begun in earnest.

Jonathan's stepfather Ken, a keen supporter but no longer a player, was at the bar getting in a round when two policemen entered. Since Sunday lunchtime stop-tap had long passed there was a respectful hush. One of the policemen shouted, 'Anyone from Trimsaran rugby club here? Someone has rung through to the station and asked us to tell you that somebody called Jonathan has been chosen for Wales.'

Ken took the congratulations by proxy and the party proceeded with an extra swing. At 5 o'clock it was suggested that they returned to Trimsaran to join the festivities there. So they bade farewell to their hosts and journeyed west. Ken doesn't quite remember how it happened but it was decided to drop in for one at the British Legion club at Loughor which was their normal port of call when returning from an away match, despite it being only fifteen miles from Trimsaran.

They were still there at 10 o'clock when Ken took a call from the Trimsaran chairman Hywel 'Titch' Richards saying that the clubhouse was packed with two coachloads of Neath fans who had come over to help Jonathan celebrate and it was embarrassing that the bulk of the Trimsaran men were still not back from a morning fixture.

It was 10.30 when they arrived back to find Trimsaran jumping. Brian Thomas and Ken Davies had gathered together quite a Neath contingent. The party went on until 3 a.m. and Jonathan did not go to work the next day.

Jonathan had shared a tear with his mother when the news first came through that morning but the sight of Ken brought a fresh onslaught of emotion which Ken found himself joining. It is in the nature of Welshmen to cry on these occasions, but for Jonathan Ken was the only senior male with whom he had shared his private dreams to have survived to see them realised. Karen's father Byron had died in front of their eyes just a few days earlier.

At least Byron had sensed that the cap was nigh. Jonathan had played in a winning Welsh 'B' team against France 'B' the previous November – the first and one of the few times Jonathan ever partnered David Bishop – and had been called up to the Welsh subs' bench for Paris.

It was not a particularly good time for a young man to come into the Welsh team. The glories of the 'seventies had died down so quickly there was scarcely an ember glowing in the Welsh hearth.

Much has been made recently of England's failure to win at Cardiff since 1963, but in 1985 a statistic of a far more worrying kind was weighing heavily on Welsh minds. Wales had lost their previous four matches at the National Stadium and were facing an historic and humiliating fifth consecutive home defeat.

▽ J.D.

I'll never forget my first game for Wales, and neither will I forget my last. And, although there were three and a half years and 27 caps between my first appearance against England and my last against Romania, I felt just the same excitement and enthusiasm for each game.

Then, after moving to Widnes, I experienced one of the greatest torments known to a Welsh international – watching Wales play without me. I watched the first three on television in the bedroom of my Widnes hotel and the last, against England, from the stand in Cardiff after an almighty fuss that led to questions in the House of Commons, but that's another story.

The point is that I shall have to think hard before I let myself attend a Welsh match again. It was not that they played badly; it is just that I am not equipped with the means to detach myself from the emotions a player goes through when he plays for Wales. I am aware that the Welsh supporters go through an intense experience as well, but unless you've been on the receiving end of all that patriotic passion you can't imagine what it is like.

You still feel it although you are not playing and the trouble is you can't respond. You want to take every pass, make every run, kick all the kicks and make every tackle. You feel totally inadequate just sitting there and old ex-internationals tell me it takes a long time for that feeling to disappear.

The first game I had to watch was Wales's match in Scotland which came only two weeks after my move north and when doubts and homesickness were still creating havoc with my peace of mind.

Today newspaper had asked me if they could do an article on my reaction to the game, so I had the company of their sportswriter

Graham Fisher in my room which is just as well, otherwise I would have cried my eyes out during the national anthem. It was odd, really. I never got paid for playing for Wales and now I was getting paid just for watching them.

But while I was watching the team as the anthem was playing, it annoyed me how many of them obviously didn't know the words. Their mouths were opening and shutting but I could tell that nothing recognisable was coming out. They looked like a row of goldfish.

Welsh is my first language but I am aware that the majority of Welshmen are brought up speaking English. And although I feel it would be great if we all could speak our national language, I accept the situation as a fact of life and I certainly don't feel that non-Welsh speakers are any less my countrymen or that their patriotism is less passionate.

But I do believe that every Welshman should be able to sing the words of his own national anthem – and if you are going to appear in front of thousands to represent the country, it becomes a duty. I am sure the lads who mumble their way through the anthem that honours the land of their fathers are as proud as any of us, but I do sense a weakening of the national fervour.

The way players sing the national anthem has much less to do with it than the way the Welsh cap has recently become devalued, in the sense that it is easier to get one.

The most capped Welsh outside halves are Cliff Morgan with 29 and Phil Bennett with 28; I come next with 27. But Cliff earned his between 1951 and 1958, a period of seven years. Phil took nine years to accumulate his. Mine came in three and a half years.

Opportunities to win caps are more frequent these days because many more countries have reached full international status. I wonder if the enthusiasm the cap generates has diminished as a result.

When caps were more difficult to win, when they were mainly limited to the four available per year in the championship, the response of the players was tremendous. Thousands of words have been written about the mystic *hwyl*, the battle spirit that invades a man when he pulls on the red shirt of Wales. It really is like having a psychological power-pack strapped to your back.

And although every detail of my first match is still vivid in my memory, what I remember most is the team spirit that day. It was the most powerful I can remember. Obviously I was younger then, and more impressionable, but it was genuinely uplifting. I had been nervous as usual but I was so fired up that my determination to succeed drove all other considerations away. Knowing Terry Holmes was a big advantage and made me much calmer. And I also reasoned that I wouldn't be there if I wasn't good enough.

When I played my last game for Wales, against Romania in Cardiff in December 1988, I felt as excited and enthusiastic as that first time. Oddly enough, the other experienced players seemed more thrilled than the new ones. As I was captain I did my best to boost everyone but the team spirit that had so impressed me three and a half years before was not as strong and certainly not as inspirational.

There were differences, admittedly. We were playing England then, and Romania certainly didn't present the same sort of challenge. And so much had happened off the field to undermine the players' respect for the hierarchy. But it was more than mere human failure. I can look back upon it now with some detachment and there's no doubt that in my comparatively short time that famous Welsh spirit lost its power to inspire every Welsh player as much as it had done. I can't prove what I say but I feel that the more caps there are the less impact they have on the players.

But I can say honestly that the thrill never lessened for me from the moment I ran out onto the National Stadium to face England that first time. It wasn't as if Wales were in a stronger position then. We had lost to Ireland and France and only narrowly defeated the wooden-spooners Scotland. Although I didn't realise it at the time, we had lost four in a row at Cardiff and a fifth defeat would have been a new record.

But defeat didn't seem a remote possibility. We were so full of confidence even a 50-yard penalty from Rob Andrew in the first minute didn't upset us. I was one of four new caps in the side. Kevin Hopkins had come into the centre, Phil Davies was at No. 8 and Gareth Roberts, who had come on as sub against France, was having his first full game as wing forward.

I imagine that, like me, they were greatly encouraged by the way experienced players like skipper Terry Holmes, Bob Norster and John Perkins attacked the game with such bite and enthusiasm.

I couldn't have asked for a better scrum half to see me through my first game than Terry. Apart from the fact that we worked for the same firm I was a great admirer of his. I have been very lucky to have played with some great scrum halves. At Neath my early days had been made much easier by having a playing partner like Carl Cnojeck, who came from Resolven and was of Polish extraction. Carl was only five feet tall but he was a hell of a player and, apart from showing me how beer should be drunk, never gave me a bad ball. He gave it quickly, too, so that I always had that extra yard.

Among Holmesy's many talents was the ability to give a long pass that is so vital for an outside half who is looking for that extra second to try something different. Before we went out for the England game, I asked him what he wanted me to do. 'Go out and play your own game,' he replied.

Our coach, the late John Bevan, also encouraged me to follow my instinct and added that if I was going to kick to make sure I put the opposition under pressure.

I did a lot of kicking that day, because I thought it would suit our game. I must admit though, it was a long time before we gained the upper hand.

My Neath team-mate Paul Thorburn had won his way into the Welsh team in the previous game against France and we were to need his accurate boot. Paul equalised Andrew's early penalty, but then England scored a try through Simon Smith which Andrew converted.

Rob Andrew played well that day and I felt my best policy was to keep driving the English pack back with kicks, just as he was trying to drive them forward. Paul kicked two penalties to equal the score again but Rob put them ahead just before half-time with another penalty.

The referee was looking at his watch, normal time had gone and he was adding on injury time, when I added my name to the scorers. We had forced our way close and I got the ball from a scrum, fairly close in but with little time, and dropped a goal. The ball only just crept over the bar but it counted and we had levelled the score at a vital time.

Rob Andrew was determined not to be upstaged that day and he dropped a left-footed goal at the start of the second half to make it 15–12 in England's favour.

But our forwards were starting to get the upper hand in their rugged battle with the English pack, and the break we had been looking for came when I hoisted a high kick towards the England line. Even as the ball left my boot I cursed because I had kicked it too far. Instead of hovering in the air and dropping in that vulnerable patch 15 yards in front of the line, the ball was arching straight towards the English full back Chris Martin. I was praised afterwards for following up so quickly, but my one thought was to get up there to retrieve what I could from my cock-up. But, under pressure from Robert Ackerman, Martin made a terrible hash of catching the ball. It spun from his grasp right into my path and all I had to do was to pounce on it to score my first try in international football.

It was a bitter blow for England and towards the end of the game I managed to set up a move that was finished off by Gareth Roberts and we came off 24–15 winners. The elation, not to mention the relief, was felt all over Wales.

As we came off the field Rob Andrew and I, as is traditional, agreed to swap shirts. Some people criticised me then and later for trying to knock Rob's head off in international matches. But if I ever went in hard against him it was only as part of the hurly burly of the game. I have never felt any animosity towards him but we are rivals, after all. Off the field I quite like him but I always feel slightly guilty when I see him.

When we agreed to exchange shirts after that first game I asked him to wait until afterwards. In the dressing room I had the Welsh substitute's shirt I had worn for the France match. It had No. 16 on the back. I gave it to him with the number hidden. He gave me his match shirt in return. In my defence I must say that I was worried it might be my first and last game for Wales and I wanted to keep the shirt. As it was, I went home to the Trimsaran celebrations next day with both the No. 10 shirts from the match.

Rob has had the decency never to mention the incident but perhaps he will forgive me when I reveal that after a match against Scotland a year or two later, I gave my shirt to their outside half who was having his first game and refused to take his in exchange. I said that as it was his first he should keep it – like I had kept mine!

My happy memories of my debut are not contradicted by the newspaper cuttings I've kept. Obviously a debut boy scoring on two crucial occasions during the game was good stuff for the headlines. I was named Man of the Match in one or two papers and generally sought out for praise. I knew how fortunate I had been with the try but, then again, I had been asked to put opponents under pressure and that's what I had done. It is a corny expression that you make your own luck but it's true. I've tried too many things that have failed unluckily not to feel justified in accepting praise for one that went my way.

And I needn't have worried about the flow of red shirts drying up. I was selected for the next game, which was against Fiji and which turned out to be very sad. Not long after it, Terry Holmes announced his decision to turn professional with Bradford Northern. I was to lose a friend, colleague and one of the best scrum halves a stand-off has ever played with.

8
Too Much, Too Fast

A year after making his international debut Jonathan had the world at his feet – and he nearly tripped over it.

In May 1986 he was voted British Player of the Year by the readers of *Rugby World*. That year he travelled a total of 80,000 miles to earn himself global recognition of his talent. He was also being carefully watched by Leeds Rugby League Club, but more of that later.

His quick, creative play not only made him outstanding for Neath and Wales but made him ideal for sevens rugby and highly suitable for those select invitation teams who love to play an open, attacking game. An impish genius is rugby's favourite animal and they had become a rarity, almost extinct.

This rush to revel in these demands for his services earned Jonathan rebuke from those who feared he might burn himself out before he had passed his mid-twenties. But how do you hold back a young man who has waited so long for the limelight? The Scottish Co-optimists, the Irish Wolfhounds, the Barbarians, were all to make flattering requests for him to join their famous ranks.

But Neath, who represented the serious side of the business, had the greatest honour for him. In the summer of 1985, when he was still only 22, they appointed him captain, the youngest in their history.

The man Jonathan was to replace was Elgan Rees, the Welsh international winger who had nursed the nervous Davies through his first class baptism three years previously. Elgan had been captain for three years and felt it was time somebody else had a go.

Brian Thomas and coach Ron Waldron had fashioned a side and

a style that was to beat the best over the next two seasons and by making Jonathan the captain they delegated the on-field control to a young brain eager and confident to lead.

All the qualities that Thomas had seen from the outset were developing fast. The exploitation of the half-gap, the tactical kicking, the defensive covering and tackling – to these were added the positive leadership required by a great team.

A passage from a report by John Billot of the *Western Mail* of a Neath–Abertillery match helps to tell the story. Neath were leading 4–3 after half an hour but not exactly setting the park alight. During an injury stoppage Jonathan decided to give them a pep-talk and Billot describes 'little Jonathan in the middle of a huddle of hulking forwards could be heard squeakily outlining his requirements – by the end of the game they had scored nine tries'.

The Neath forwards responded to him because, as pack leader Mike Richards explained at the time, 'our forwards know that good, hard-won ball is not going to be wasted and that when they win possession they are going to be moving forward with it'.

This attacking style led to a rush of tries from forwards as well as backs. At one time in this period Neath were averaging four tries a match, thanks mainly to Jonathan's imaginative ability to create gaps for those around him as well as for himself.

But by the end of that season Neath fans were narked that they hadn't seen enough of him. What with international calls and round-the-world trips for sevens tournaments, Jonathan did not play for Neath that season after early March. But his last two games left the Gnoll with enough contentment to last a couple of months as Jonathan lead Neath to home victories against Pontypool and Bristol in four days.

Pontypool were the reigning Welsh champions but Neath completed the double over them with a 16–12 victory which owed much to a penalty try awarded when Jonathan was impeded as he chased after a kick for what would have been a certain try. Then Bristol arrived on their first visit to Neath for 13 years and were plastered 38–0 as Jonathan opened them up like a tin of beans.

The international season, his first full championship, confirmed the promise. Against Ireland in Dublin, Wales were trailing until Jonathan brilliantly created a try that led to victory. At Twickenham, Rob Andrew stole the show by scoring a record 21 points to give England a 21–19 win but it was Davies who caught the connoisseur's eye by cheekily endeavouring to attack from drop-outs from his own twenty-five. He then helped to beat Scotland with blistering surges from deep inside his own half, 'rekindling,' said one writer, 'a vitality which many had thought had disappeared into some other world of Celtic mist'.

He was in the Welsh team to play in the Sydney Sevens and he commanded most of the praise despite some exalted company. New Zealand were the inevitable winners but the sheen of their triumph was dulled because Wales beat them in the pool game early in the tournament, with Jonathan scoring three tries in 14 minutes against them. It has been a long time since anyone has done that in any form of rugby.

Wales also beat France, Tonga and the United States before losing to Australia in the semi-final – a game they still think they could have won. In all Jonathan scored seven tries and although there was no official Man of the Tournament award, he was generally hailed as the outstanding player on view.

Alan Jones, the Australian coach who made such an impact on world rugby, called him a cocky little bugger which no doubt passes for praise in that country. Australian TV commentators, not accustomed nor inclined to lavish praise on Britons, described his tries with words like 'sensational' and 'absolutely dynamic'. The tournament did more for his reputation than all his previous performances put together.

While he was in Sydney he had an offer to play for the Irish Wolfhounds in the Hong Kong Sevens a few weeks later. That meant coming home, playing for the Barbarians against Cardiff on Easter Saturday and then returning to the Far East. Then he heard he'd been selected for the British Lions to play against the Rest of the World at Twickenham.

It was all too much, of course, a fact gravely commented upon by Bleddyn Williams, one of the most respected of all former Welsh rugby heroes, who warned in the *Sunday People*:

'Jonathan Davies can become the greatest fly-half in the world . . . but he must learn to say "No" now and again or he'll disappear even faster than he arrived.'

Bleddyn went on to describe the rush which began with the 20,000 mile round trip to Australia.

Six days later he was the mastermind as the Barbarians beat Cardiff and then he flew another 15,000 miles to play in the Hong Kong

87

Sevens for an Irish team. It is hardly surprising that a hamstring injury keeps him out of the British Lions *v.* The Rest match.

Davies will not spend the summer taking a breather. He'll be off to Fiji, Tonga and Western Samoa as the only fly-half in the Welsh touring party. Wales are relying on 23-year-old Davies to survive all this and lead them to what could be the start of another golden era.

There is no doubt he has all the talent and charisma of former heroes Barry John and Phil Bennett. In Australia his superb performances sent highly critical writers and fans into ecstasies. Mark Ella, the brilliant Australian fly-half who destroyed British rugby with the Wallabies last year, was captivated by Davies. Ella is the greatest fly-half of modern times, and for him to rave about young Davies is praise indeed. But Ella has now retired – far too early – because he was unable to cope with the pressures of today's rugby. He found his private life was non-existent and eventually he became totally disillusioned with the game. That's what "the hottest property in world rugby" must avoid.

▽ J.D.

Apart from being one of the greatest backs ever to pull on a Welsh jersey, Bleddyn Williams writes a lot of sense as a journalist and there is no doubt he was right when he criticised my crowded rugby life in 1986. I was doing too much, too fast. But I was young and eager.

What he didn't know was that I was complicating my life even further by having secret meetings with Harry Jepson, the chairman of Leeds Rugby League Football Club. Harry is a respected and popular figure in rugby league and I soon discovered why. Not only has his long association with the game, and with watching union, made him a very knowledgeable man, he is also very likeable and as straight as they come.

He became interested in trying to persuade me to move north after watching my debut for Wales against England and kept tabs on me whenever he could get down to South Wales. We once met in the Ivy Bush Royal Hotel in Carmarthen and he showed me a cheque made out to me for £30,000. 'That's just the down payment,' he said. I'll never forget it, I was eating minestrone soup at the time.

On another occasion Harry arrived in Cardiff for a meeting with me and, since he was a little early, wandered down to Cardiff Arms Park to see if he could have a look around. He strolled onto the pitch where someone asked if they could help him. He explained he was down from the north and wanted to see the famous stadium. They showed him around and, up above the pitch, he could see the Welsh RU secretary Ray Williams in his office. Harry wondered if they would have been so hospitable if they'd known he was trying to entice their outside half away.

Harry was a very persuasive man and was adamant, both to me and his board back at Leeds, that I would be ideal for the league code. He scoffed at suggestions that I wouldn't be big enough. The finest stand-off he'd ever seen was a Welshman called Oliver Morris from Pontypridd. Oliver weighed 9st 6lbs and went north in 1937. After he was rejected by Warrington, Harry helped to get him a chance at Hunslet where Oliver was a key figure when they won the Championship in 1938. Oliver joined the Welch Regiment when the war started and was killed in action, otherwise Harry reckons he would have become one of the greats.

Although I was having a great time enjoying the fruits of my new success in union I must admit that Harry's interest was making me think very hard about my future. The old word security began to enter my thoughts. Leeds were offering £100,000 tax free which for a 23-year-old in 1986 was a fair lump of money and was £20,000 more than Terry Holmes was reputed to have received from Bradford Northern a few months earlier.

It was Terry's departure that first sowed the seeds. We had worked together and had long conversations about rugby and its effect on our lives. We came from similar working class backgrounds and had been fortunate in finding an employer like Neil. But what of the long-term future?

Even then, when he decided to go it was a shock to me. At the age of 28 he was captain of Cardiff, one of the greatest clubs in the world, captain of Wales and a British Lion. And here he was, turning his back on all that and leaving his beloved home city in order to get some more tangible reward from his rugby before it was too late.

Terry had achieved things in rugby union that even someone as ambitious as I didn't even dare dream about, and in the end he had to pack his bags and leave in order to earn some financial security for himself and his family. Terry may not have seen it quite in that light but it is how I saw it and it troubled me.

At the beginning of the 1986–87 season Leeds invited me and Karen to pay a visit to the club and have a look around. I wanted to see a rugby league match in the flesh. I had never seen one before although I was an avid viewer of televised matches. There was a Yorkshire Cup game between Featherstone and Hull KR and Harry took us down. It was a sell-out and the only accommodation they could give us was in one of their new executive boxes in their rebuilt stand.

The box was glass-sided and it was like being in a goldfish bowl. Rugby league folk are no less nosey than anyone else and the directors of both sides and all the officials in the stand were craning to see who Harry had with him. He explained later that I was a friend from Australia but when the match was over Harry hesitated before going into the Portacabin that was serving as a temporary board room while the stand was being finished.

'All the national press will be in there, they're bound to recognise you,' he said.

I replied that I didn't feel I was committing a crime just by watching a game. So in we went. Harry introduced me as his friend John and all the reporters shook hands but obviously had no idea who I was.

After I'd signed for Widnes, Harry had great pleasure in saying to those same press boys that he was surprised they were making so much fuss about Jonathan Davies when they'd ignored me completely a few years earlier when he'd introduced me to them!

I came so close to signing for Leeds I often wonder how my career would have gone. Harry is convinced I would have been a great success but I am not so sure. The three extra years I spent in union helped to mature me and make me more confident mentally and physically. As a 23-year-old I am not sure I would have been able to withstand the pressures on my body and my morale as well as I did when I eventually came north.

Once I had made my mind up to go to Widnes, Harry was the first person I rang. He was gracious enough to say I was going to a great club and wish me all the best.

Had I gone to Leeds in '86 I couldn't have placed my future in better hands than Harry's and the club's coach Peter Fox. But the good time I was having was too strong an anchor. And although Bleddyn Williams was undoubtedly right to warn of the risks, how could I reject the chances of seeing the world that came pouring in?

They started soon after I'd made my debut for Wales in 1985. First came the Co-optimists, the famous Scottish invitation side who were due to play in Zimbabwe. Suddenly I was flying to play in Africa with players like the legendary Irish forward Moss Keane and

I was coming home with stories that had them wide-eyed in the Trimsaran clubhouse. What a sight Moss was when he tried to learn to swim on that trip; he was so petrified of water he'd taken a good drink which didn't help his efforts to keep his 19 stones afloat. While we were in Zimbabwe we were taken to a safari park where our coach stopped in the lion compound for us to get out and walk about. The lions, we were told, were quite tame. All of a sudden one of them attacked a little boy who was there with his parents. Before the lion could do any damage, Hugh McHardy ran up and kicked the lion so hard it turned its attention on us. The sight of 30 rugby players trying to get back into a coach at the same time must be fresh in those lions' minds even now.

After the Co-optimists I was invited to play in a World Sevens tournament in South Africa, in a team that also included Australians David Campese, Glen Ella and Roger Gould. Once more I was in class company, although I found the socialising didn't help the rugby very much. It was a great experience, however, and brought me face to face with apartheid for the first time.

I walked into a crowded bar with Glen Ella and was about to start jostling my way through when the crowd parted as if by magic. We walked up to the bar with ease. Then it dawned on me – Glen is an aborigine and what we were experiencing was the opposite of a friendly welcome. People preferred to leave rather than drink in the same bar as a coloured person. I was horrified and we got merrily pissed together, almost as an act of defiance.

South Africa is one of the great rugby playing nations of the world, they may even be the greatest, but an experience like that must cloud the views of every sportsman who visits there. I've never been back but whenever there's been an invitation in the offing I have to admit the challenge of pitting my rugby skills against theirs has been a temptation.

Although, I might steer clear of Durban even if I did go. I went to a doctor there to see if he could help ease the pain and discomfort I was getting from piles. He went to work with a scalpel, without giving me an anaesthetic, and I doubt if the memory will ever leave me.

Back home the honour of being made captain of Neath took me into the new season with great enthusiasm. Brian Thomas had got the club buzzing and we were fast becoming a team no-one in the country relished meeting. Our try-scoring rate was tremendous and with our pack winning so much ball all options open to me gave me an exciting freedom.

I was chosen to play for Wales against Fiji, which was to be Terry Holmes's last international, and by the time the Championship matches came around I was teamed up with a new scrum half, Robert Jones of Swansea, who was to become a firm friend and ally in 25 Welsh matches.

When Wales decided to enter a team in the inaugural Sydney Sevens I was delighted. Brian Thomas says I like sevens rugby because I like showing off. I'm not sure about that, but I do like running with the ball and in sevens you get plenty of chance for that. Considering it was our first attempt we did very well to reach the semi-final where we were beaten by Australia. We all agreed that with a little more experience, we would have selected a team more suited to playing against the Aussies and might have beaten them.

But it was a great two days for all that and I came out of it with seven tries, three of them against the All Blacks, and worldwide recognition. I also learned a great deal from watching great players at work. I particularly remember Serge Blanco, the great French full back. I found that Serge was following my positioning on the field. If I was at centre, so was he. If I appeared on the wing, then he followed. He was marking me, an unknown. I should have been shadowing him. It was an object lesson on how a top player approaches his duties on the field and I learned a lot from it. As it happened we beat France 12–8 in the quarter final match and Serge didn't stop me scoring a try. Then again, where was I when he scored his?

After I returned to make my debut for the Barbarians, I was soon packing to join the Irish Wolfhounds on their trip to the Hong Kong Sevens. My team-mates included Hugo McNeil, Willie Anderson, Brendan Mullin and Michael Kiernan. Any trip with the Irish is likely to be good fun and since I had been in the Welsh team who had beaten Ireland in Dublin a few months earlier there was plenty of added banter.

I had played more sevens rugby than they had, so I was the sort of general. Unfortunately, I pulled a hamstring in our second game, which was entirely due to the socialising demanded of anyone who plays with the Irish, and that was the end of the competition for me.

It was also the end of my chances of playing for the British Lions *v.* The Rest of the World at Cardiff on my return, or for the Five Nations team *v.* The Overseas at Twickenham three days later. I was sorry not to get my British Lions cap; I would have been devastated had I known that I would never get another chance to play for them.

The hamstring mended in time for me to join Wales on their tour of Fiji, Tonga and Western Samoa, but I had to take a strict fitness test before we left. There were times in the next couple of months when I wished I'd failed it.

Arriving in Fiji proved to be an immediate embarrassment. They are avid watchers of rugby on television and film of the Sydney Sevens had been played over and over again. 'Davees, Davees,' they chanted as we came down the steps of the 'plane. I was not allowed to forget that by the boys for the rest of the visit.

The hotel was nice, the weather was sweltering and the rugby was just about the hardest any of us had encountered. David Pickering, who had been captain of our sevens team in Sydney, was kicked on the head in the first game and it was one of the most frightening things I've seen on the field. There was blood coming out of his mouth, his nose and his ears. He refused to go off but it was clear that it was a very nasty injury. The next day it was decided that he should go back home and when we saw him off he had such a distant look in his eyes we were all very worried. I think it took him a long time to get over that injury.

We won our Test match against Fiji by 21–15 and I managed to score a try. But before we left we played a game of touch rugby against the Fijian army and they slaughtered us. It was like playing the Harlem Globetrotters.

The people were very friendly, forever wanting to buy us drinks or share their bottles with us. It was so hot we tended to drink more than we should have. One night one of our officials decided to come out for a drink and show us how real drinking was done. He was so drunk at the end we took all his clothes off and we arrived at the hotel with him at the front of the bus singing 'Are you Lonesome Tonight?'. As he stepped off the bus, still stark naked and still singing, the rest of the official party were arriving back from a function. It was a hilarious confrontation.

We flew from Fiji to Tonga which are called the Friendly Isles for a reason that did not become apparent, although I must admit we probably saw them at their least attractive. We feared the worst at the airport when our baggage arrived in a trailer attached to the back of a tractor and was handed to us through a hole in the wall. It seemed as if the entire island had turned out to greet us; they just stood there quietly studying us. It was pouring with rain which didn't stop for eight days. Neither did the mosquitoes. And the number of transvestites there is embarrassing. You try refusing a 15-stone man wearing lipstick and a dress when he asks you to dance.

And if we thought the rugby was tough in Fiji, we had seen nothing. In the first game against the President's XV I kicked ahead and saw this horizontal man come flying at me. They literally come at you like Exocet missiles and this fella's head hit me in the middle of the chest so hard I went down like a sack of potatoes. I always try to jump back up after being hit, so that it doesn't look as if they've hurt me. But as I got to my feet, I fell straight back down again. I felt as if every muscle in my chest was contracting and I could hardly breathe. I tried to stay on and I even kicked a drop goal from the next scrum but I had to go off.

I had so much trouble breathing they decided to send me to hospital. Mark Titley, the Swansea winger, came with me and I was very pleased he did. My chest was in such a state I thought I was dying. I have to confess that I was crying on the way to the hospital, I really thought my time had come.

We had changed at the hotel, so I was still in my kit as we sat in the waiting-room. No-one came to see us so, still finding it hard to breathe, I found a room marked 'Casualty' and walked in. There was a man in there listening to a transistor radio. 'I'm sorry,' he said. 'Everybody's at the game.'

We sat down and listened to the game together for a while until I told him how terrible I felt and that I needed attention. He went away and came back with two aspirins. Mark didn't feel it was worth us staying there any more so we returned to the hotel.

The following day the King of Tonga himself sent a message apologising and insisted I went back to the hospital for an X-ray. I was feeling better but still a bit groggy, so I went. Jeff Whitefoot, the big Cardiff prop, came with me. He'd had an insect bite on his elbow which had swollen up and was looking decidedly nasty. There didn't seem to be any doors in the hospital and people and dogs were just wandering in to have a look at us. Then a girl came along to look at Jeff's arm. She took out a scalpel and Jeff caught hold of my hand. They may look tough these forwards but they can be babies like the rest of us.

She just sliced through the big lump on Jeff's elbow like an apple and proceeded to squeeze the pus out. I don't know who was making more noise, Jeff or me, because he was crushing my hand so hard I thought the bones were going to be powdered. Still, it seemed to cheer up everyone in the hospital.

Then came the Test match against Tonga and we braced ourselves for a battle. We didn't brace hard enough. We should have known what to expect when we accidentally broke one of the windows in the dressing room and the police burst in and tried to arrest Stuart Evans and Phil Davies. This was war.

We won the game 15–9 and lost the fights 6–1. At one time or another six of our men were laid flat out by punches. I managed to avoid catching one of them but Adrian Hadley wasn't so lucky. He was so spark out, they drove the ambulance on to the pitch to take him off to hospital. Phil Davies was flattened from behind by the Tongan No. 8 Emosi Koloto, who happens to be a team-mate of mine at Widnes now, so we laugh about it. Oddly enough, the prop who hit Adrian had played against Wales the day Adrian, Mark Ring and myself played in the Under-12's curtain-raiser in 1974.

At one time I said to the referee, 'If you don't do something somebody's going to get killed.' It wasn't in any way due to him that everyone survived the match.

The next day both teams were taken on a boat trip, with half our team nursing sore jaws while the Tongans were as happy and friendly as if the match had never happened. That evening at the farewell dinner the King made a speech in the Tongan language and our people thought it would be nice if we replied in Welsh, so they asked me. I must confess that I took advantage of the fact that none of the Tongans and few of our own party could speak Welsh. I said that it hadn't stopped raining since we got there. We didn't like the food. They'd tried to kill us on the pitch and we couldn't wait to get home. A Welsh interpreter could have caused a major diplomatic incident.

We went from there to Western Samoa which we had been warned was the worst place of the three. It turned out to be the best. Good weather, good hotel, good food, a good pitch and the cleanest game. And I had the pleasure of playing against Michael Jones, the great All Black wing forward of Welsh descent I would have to face up to two years later under entirely different circumstances.

95

9
Trouble and Strife

After a year in which glory and praise flowed past him like a river in flood, Jonathan entered 1987 fully justified in his feeling that he had arrived as a major force in world rugby and that he was held in the highest esteem by his fellow countrymen. But by the end of the year he was close to having seen every part of his newly-found status dismantled.

He still produced great moments, and his back still felt the odd hearty slap, but the year was blackened by a series of events that piled trouble upon trouble. In chronological order they were:

— A magazine interview in which Jonathan freely admitted his dissatisfaction with the lack of financial reward from union for the hard work put in by players and said that he would probably 'go north' sooner or later. The Welsh Rugby Union accused him of professionalising himself as a result.

— His marriage to Karen hit a rocky spell and they separated. While they were apart he met another girl who was to accuse him of being a 'Rugby Rat' on the front page of the *Daily Mirror*.

— He fell out with Brian Thomas because he refused to commit himself to future seasons with Neath, and he left to join Llanelli under a cloud of rumour and suspicion.

— Wales won only one match in the Championship and although they finished a highly creditable third in the World Cup, Jonathan was criticised for not living up to expectations.

— He missed a Welsh international match against the USA through injury and the good performance of his replacement Bleddyn Bowen led to calls for Wales to have a less individually flamboyant outside half than Jonathan.

– Returning from a funeral he crashed into a lamp-post and was subsequently charged with drunken driving.

It was a catalogue of calamity from which a more vulnerable spirit might not have emerged at all. Jonathan was able to cling on to his self-belief because of its strong roots and because, deep down, the realisation began to dawn slowly that his problems stemmed solely from the loss of his stable relationship with Karen.

But while that was sinking in to a mind preoccupied with the responsibilities and celebrations of success, circumstances started to conspire against him. The early maturity that had enabled him to cope with the devastations and disappointments of his youth seemed inadequate to handle the difficulties of his sudden status.

Success, however, did not go to his head, it went to his mouth. Not in a boastful way but in the sense that it caused him to come out with comments and opinions that may have perhaps been better left unsaid or whispered to a trusted few. But he has always been frank and forthright and he saw no danger in continuing to be so despite the dramatic upsurge in the number of eager listeners.

He was outspoken, in particular, in his impatience with the lack of earning potential in union and it was only a matter of time before this would reach unsympathetic ears.

In December 1986 I invited him to the Sports Writers' Association annual awards presentation dinner at Wembley. His demeanour was not that of an arrogant young sports hero revelling in being part of a dinner-suited celebrity evening. His lack of sophistication, or even any pretence of it, was evident as his eyes took on that stargazer's swivel, sweeping around tables studded with the top sports people of the moment.

He is very knowledgeable on most sports and afterwards he was darting about talking to his favourites. I expected the autograph book to appear any minute. He had a long chat with Roger Black the athlete and returned marvelling at the fact that in athletics, for so long as strictly amateur as rugby union, money could be earned as long as it was paid into a trust fund for when they retired.

'He doesn't have to work, he can train all the time. And he knows that when he packs it in he'll have the benefit of what his running has earned,' he said, enviously.

Although he was warned by more than one person to modify his public pronouncements on the matter of getting paid for playing rugby, Jonathan found discretion hard to come by. It wasn't long before he spoke at length to journalist Peter Bills who arrived to do a lengthy article about him in a new magazine called *Sportsweek* launched by the Maxwell empire.

It was a very well presented piece and in it Jonathan spoke at great length about the shortcomings of rugby union, and Welsh rugby union in particular, and how if someone came along with £100,000 plus a car and a house he could be persuaded to play rugby league and that's where he would end up sooner or later. In fact, the article quoted him as saying it was 99 per cent certain he would go.

For a rugby union player it was as eloquent a suicide note as could be imagined and the press took up the story with the biggest megaphones they could find.

Not surprisingly, the WRU announced an investigation into whether Jonathan had professionalised himself by so directly announcing his availability to rugby league clubs. The laws relating to professionalism in union are very strict and even talking to a league club is enough to lose a player his amateur status. Jonathan couldn't have advertised his willingness to go if he'd put a card in every newsagent's shop window in Lancashire.

Jonathan is not the first person to realise that words spoken over a nice lunch take on extra impact in cold and unforgiving print and, fearing that he was about to be drummed out of the game, wrote an immediate letter of apology and appeared before them in person for his 'unguarded statements' which were 'taken out of context and manipulated for sensationalism'.

Ironically, while the furore was going on, Mr Maxwell decided to close down *Sportsweek* magazine in the same week that Jonathan was also hovering over the same plug-hole.

But Jonathan did have one persuasive argument on his side. He was the best outside half in the world and Wales were not only about to play the Five Nations Championships but the first World Cup was taking place in May. Had he been a more expendable player an example might well have been made, but the WRU accepted his explanation and decided to take no further action, apart from strongly refuting any suggestion that top Welsh players were being poorly treated and that the administrators were out of touch. Since the accusation is still being made, even more strongly, to this day, perhaps they should have done more reflecting than refuting.

There are many who suggest that Jonathan did not get off scot-free, that his punishment was not to be awarded the captaincy that many were campaigning for on his behalf. He was making a success of leading Neath and was such a central and assertive figure in the Welsh team, it seemed an obvious move – but not once he had announced himself a rebel.

What might have happened to him – or indeed to Wales who were about to lose all but one of their four Championship games – had he kept his mouth shut and been given the captaincy is fascinating to consider. The honour might well have stabilised him at a time when he was starting to show the signs of restlessness that have affected so many young sports stars. A steadying responsibility at that moment could have calmed the impatience that fractured his marriage and led to his falling out with Neath.

Certainly he could have done no more on the rugby field to deserve being given the leadership of Wales. Brian Thomas had seen him develop and mature as Neath's captain and was eager to endorse Jonathan's candidature. 'He is a rugby genius and it is annoying that it has taken people four years to realise it,' he told the press.

'He dictates every game, deciding exactly what the game is going to do. He is a leader in every sense. With Jonathan it is almost like playing chess on the rugby field. He is three moves ahead of the game. If people can't see that, they must be blind.'

It was a view supported by Neath's former captain Elgan Rees who said, 'We have got to expand our game if we are going to do well in the World Cup and Jonathan is perfectly placed to call the right moves. He is the right man at the right moment.'

Jonathan had missed the start of that season with a recurrence of the hamstring injury incurred in the hectic end to the previous season. It had not gone unnoticed that he had played in only half the matches in that season but as the WRU had asked their World Cup squad not to overtax themselves in the 1986–87 season, injuries were given plenty of time to heal and he had missed six weeks when he returned for a match against South Wales Police.

Once again he proved his ability to play after a long absence without displaying the slightest physical or mental rustiness. He scored a try and his imagination and speed proved to be the main difference between the two sides as Neath won 30–17.

Then he faced Pontypool, the reigning champions, at the Gnoll and the result was two tries and two drop goals to crown a performance one writer nominated as 'one of the best individual performances turned in at club level in the past ten years'. Neath's strong and mobile team-play gave him the ammunition he needed to completely control the game.

The nearest any team came to breaking Neath's unbeaten home record that season was Bridgend who by half-time had built a 13–9 lead to stun the Gnoll into a nervous silence. The Bridgend captain Adrian Owen recalled: 'Our up-and-unders had them worried and our scrum was doing its job. We were in a very strong position – then Jonathan decided to play and there was no way we were going to stop him. He made up his mind about how he was going to score his try three moves ahead. He set everything up until the scrum was near enough – then zoom.' Neath won 22–13.

But it was the game against Bath that brought him national attention. Neath had taken Bath's ground record the previous season but Bath, who had later won the John Player Cup for the third consecutive year, had enhanced their standing as England's top club and were determined to get revenge.

The press, not unnaturally, billed the confrontation as the battle to decide the best club in Britain. If this was true then there was not much doubt about which team could claim the title – Neath scored a comprehensive 26–9 victory after which Jonathan was variously hailed as genius, a destroyer and a showman, 'perhaps the finest game of his sensational career' wrote John Billot of the *Western Mail*.

He rarely put a foot wrong, choosing the precise time when it was right to chip ahead, to find a long touch, to pass, to dart through on his own. And he added a devastating touchline tackle on Bath winger Tony Swift. He dropped a goal in the second half and a little later shaped to drop another. But it was just a feint, and in a flash he was around the blindside, cutting past five defenders before diving, a touch flamboyantly, over the line. It was a try shown over and over again on television and watched with interest in places like St. Helens, Widnes and Leeds.

Even those used to seeing him marvelled at that performance. Geoffrey Nicholson of the *Independent* wrote: 'Even after one full international season Davies still looks like a schoolboy who has been promoted to senior rugby. You worry for him . . . but the memory most will have carried away was the subtle mastery of the Neath stand-off.'

It was Jonathan's best period of sustained brilliance at club level. He scored a try in 42 seconds against Coventry. Against Llanelli in the Schweppes Cup he scored three dropped goals and hit the post with another. 'Davies dominated the game,' grumbled Llanelli coach Gareth Jenkins.

The Times profiled him under the headline, 'A god to rouse the Valleys'. Jacques Fouroux, the French coach, christened him 'the Diego Maradona of World Rugby'.

This fame, however, was not to be nourished by the Five Nations Championships. The only win Wales managed was against England, inevitably, at Cardiff. The Welsh pack were unable to win enough good ball to bring their backs into the game with sufficient frequency. But, generally, the chemistry was not working. The defeats against Ireland in Cardiff, Scotland at Murrayfield and France in Paris were not by large margins, and a couple could have gone either way, but three beatings out of four was not a major boost to their World Cup hopes.

But Jonathan was up to his neck in other worries. His marital trouble was a slowly developing wound in his morale and was hardly helped by the breakdown of his relationship with Brian Thomas.

Jonathan had come to mean a great deal to Neath, far more than a good player normally does to a club. He had been the hub of the side, achieving on the pitch what Brian Thomas had achieved off it. Thomas was undoubtedly the architect of Neath's success but Davies was the master craftsman.

The club estimate that his presence alone could put 40 per cent on the attendance figures which were already swollen by the sort of play that rattled up 113 tries in 22 wins out of 25 games. People would ring up to see if he was playing before setting out for the game. As one of his illustrious predecessors Phil Bennett said: 'If you knew Jonathan was playing for Neath even bad weather wouldn't keep you indoors.'

This applied even on away matches. Jonathan once travelled up to Blackheath with the Neath team but, since he had a slight strain, it was decided to rest him. During the first half he was sitting in the bar with his feet up, drinking a pint and watching a rugby league match on television when a group of men came in. They told him they'd driven a long way to watch him and were sorry he wasn't able to play. While they were talking one of the Neath backs was injured. He finished his pint, went down to the dressing rooms and turned out for the second half.

But there came a point when Brian Thomas began to get alarmed at the vibes he was getting from Jonathan's direction. There had been rumours in the previous season that Cardiff were interested in persuading Jonathan to play for them. After all, he did work for a Cardiff firm. But nothing came of them and Jonathan pledged himself to Neath for the following season.

Now the rumours were starting up again. He was obviously unsettled because of his marriage problems and the *Sportsweek* article had hardly demonstrated a man whose future was firmly welded to the union code. Other rumours had spoken of his playing in France, Italy and Australia.

A team manager as thorough as Brian Thomas knows that no team is more vulnerable than one containing an exceptional player. Superstars can do wonders but they leave big holes behind them when they go as many a team, soccer and rugby, have learned in the past.

If Jonathan was leaving, Brian wanted to know immediately. He wanted to start the reorganisation that the side would have to undergo to retain its impetus. So he questioned Jonathan about his future.

When the player said he hadn't thought about it, Thomas asked for a commitment to Neath for at least the following season. Jonathan protested that he wasn't thinking past the World Cup, that there was no need for this showdown.

Neath, who had been knocked out of the Schweppes Cup in the semi-finals by Cardiff, but who won the Merit Table, shocked the rugby world by announcing at the end of April: 'Because he has failed to make his future intentions clear, Jonathan Davies can no longer be considered as part of the progression plan of Neath RFC. Whatever code, country or club he will be involved with in future Neath RFC wishes him the best of luck.' Stuart Evans was named as the new captain.

Everyone was stunned but no more than Jonathan, who didn't know where the hell he was going. Without a wife, without a club, he made ready for the World Cup in Australasia.

▽ J.D.

It is common knowledge in Wales that I left Neath because I wanted a share of the gate money and they wouldn't give it to me. So I went to Llanelli because they offered £300 a week and a share of the car park takings.

If you talked around the bars and clubs of South Wales I am sure you would find other versions of my reasons for changing clubs but that's my favourite because if it was true I would never have moved to Widnes. Llanelli have got a very big car park.

Whether it is big enough to pay for all the players it is reputed to pay I shall have to leave the AA and the Inland Revenue to work out.

Ever since it became known that we were writing this book, people have been sidling up to me asking, 'Are you going to take the lid off?' or 'Are you going to spill the beans?'.

Well, I'm very happy to take the lid off, but I don't think you'll find many beans.

I'll tell you exactly what I received from Llanelli. They gave me £50 a month for expenses, which just covered my petrol costs for the 90 miles a week I travelled, and £10 for a drink after each match. I didn't take much change home.

That's how much I received, no more, no less and it is roughly equivalent to what I received from Neath. And from what I know about Cardiff, Swansea and Newport, their players get about the same.

I realise this will be a major disappointment because stories about the vast amounts of money paid to Welsh rugby union players have become an accepted fact of life. The week after I moved to Widnes the former England scrum half Steve Smith said in a speech to the Rugby Writers' Association: 'Jonathan Davies is the first player to go North and take a pay cut.'

It's a good joke and I've used it myself several times since. I'm told that at a dinner in the 'seventies a speaker compared Llanelli with Leeds United, the soccer giants of the time. 'They get paid more than Leeds,' cried a voice from the back.

As embedded in our minds as these impressions are I am afraid I must be disappointing and say that I never came across payment to players. There are other payments I shall reveal – but money from clubs to players for playing I have never come across personally.

There will be some who say that I'm obeying the honourable code of silence by which former players protect their friends who are still drawing the illegal cash. If such a code existed I can't imagine it lasting long. Too many players leave clubs with grudges not to be tempted to blow the gaffe, especially with the tabloid press anxious to pay good money for dirt.

And since I am heavily critical of the hypocrisy of rugby union, I can assure you I would not pass up a chance to present personal evidence of it, friends or no friends.

I am not saying categorically that no player in Welsh rugby has ever been paid or is being paid. I've got my suspicions like everyone else. As a matter of fact I was offered £15 a week by a West Wales club four years before I joined Llanelli.

Clubs trying to make headway, unfashionable clubs stuck up the end of a valley where they get frost in September — these are the ones who may find it necessary to attract a better standard of player by being over-generous with the expenses. But I doubt if you are talking about more than £50–£100 for the odd player, because that sort of club couldn't afford any more unless they had a wealthy benefactor willing to pay sums out of his own pocket.

But the major clubs, as far as I know, merely look after their players as well as they can within the rules. Players joining them know they will have the best kit, a good standard of travelling and hotel comfort and good facilities plus the job benefits that go with belonging to a famous club.

Most players put up with the rumours in a good-natured way because the more you protest the more they disbelieve you. But there is another side to it that isn't funny. The attitude of spectators to players is affected by this belief that large sums of money are being earned. They feel entitled to abuse you if you perform below expectations, if they feel you are not worth the money you are supposed to get paid. So you lose in two ways. And a player putting everything into rugby and getting nothing out of it but criticism is likely to wonder if it is all worth it.

Having dispensed with cash as a reason for my leaving Neath to join Llanelli, I shall ignore the several other lurid theories that were bandied about at the time – that I'd had a fight with Brian Thomas, that Karen had made it a condition of our reconciliation and so on.

The main reason why all these theories about my decision are wrong, is that I didn't make a decision. It was made for me.

Looking back on what happened I still can't quite believe it. I can understand Brian's concern about having an early warning of any departure and I have to admit that it wasn't one of the most secure periods of my life, but I really wasn't sure what I was going to do.

I realise that I'd made public my feelings about an eventual move to rugby league and there was other speculation about me going abroad to play union, but there were no plans in the offing otherwise I would have told him when he asked me.

But once he gave me the ultimatum that I had to commit myself to Neath there and then, it immediately made me think about it. How did I know what was around the corner? Tell me any other rugby union player who has ever given an undertaking he wouldn't leave a club for a certain period.

There are very few advantages in being an amateur rugby player and one of them is the freedom to play for who the hell you please, providing the necessary permits or permissions have been received. There are no contracts from season to season.

All I had in mind that precise time, apart from my personal problems, was going to the World Cup. It had entered my head that I might be playing somewhere other than Neath when I returned but to create a confrontation over such a small doubt practically ensured my departure. I had enough on my plate, why was I suddenly being hemmed in by ultimatums? What if there was a league club ready to offer me a great deal, would I have to say sorry but I've given Neath a commitment? But I respected his point of view in his capacity as a manager.

I think Brian sensed that I would go to league sooner or later, and if he was going to have to replace me he would prefer to do it when he had plenty of time to reorganise, rather than be caught on the hop by a sudden decision.

But it was two years before I turned professional with Widnes; had that confrontation never happened I could have spent that time with Neath. There is no question in my mind about that.

I had thought of Llanelli during the season but only after Neath had shown me the door did I really consider the Scarlets as an ideal place for me to go. I have never regretted going there, even though it was not all smooth at first.

They were the club I had been brought up on, where all my boyhood heroes played, where my own father played, where my brother-in-law was captain and it was very close to where I live. I could have gone to Cardiff or other clubs but Stradey was so obvious it didn't need thinking about.

But Llanelli had once rejected me while Neath had given me my big chance. I still have my doubts if I would have deserted the Gnoll for Stradey had they not voluntarily released me from my allegiance to them.

There were ill-feelings at the time but only because the true facts weren't known. I just hope the Neath people don't still hold it against me. I don't regret joining Llanelli where I think I became the better player.

I suppose a lot of my trouble in 1987 could be traced to that article in *Sportsweek*. I've never been one to hide my feelings or disguise my real opinions. If I get asked anything I usually answer with exactly what's in my mind. I try to be a little more diplomatic these days but I was less mature then and I did feel very strongly about my plight as a so-called star who was facing a future as poor as his past.

Had I seen it all laid out as it was in the magazine I might have protested. It filled page after page. No wonder the WRU took exception. I am lucky I didn't get drop-kicked up north. But I reckon I paid a big penalty. If, as they say, I missed being chosen as captain of Wales at that time it could have been very costly in terms of opportunity and experience. And perhaps Brian would never have felt the need to tie me down if he hadn't read those words.

I owed everything to Neath and if that article prevented me from repaying the debt in full, it was a very costly mistake.

10
Failed Playboy

Jonathan's favourite sportsmen are George Best, Alex Higgins, Ian Botham and John McEnroe, each of whom is or was largely an instinctive performer, an untamed sporting spirit able to suddenly infuse his game with brilliant and audacious action. It may be just a coincidence that each in his own way is also powered by other unpredictable characteristics that have often led to trouble.

For skilful impetuosity on the field of play, Jonathan obviously bears comparison with his heroes, but he hardly qualifies to be included in the same category for their other activities. There are traces of rebellion in his nature and when there's been a touch of after-match hell-raising to be done he wouldn't allow himself to be discounted as a contributor, but as a sporting playboy he falls well short of the required standard.

Even his brief dalliance with that sort of existence floundered on a lack of natural talent for the wild life.

He'd been fond of a drink of beer since his Trimsaran days. When the clubhouse is a converted pub and when club business is invariably transacted in the bar then rugby and beer tend to become inseparable, especially on a Saturday night when it is as important to hold your own with a glass as it was with a ball.

After he'd joined Neath, one of the drinking friends he developed was a 6ft 3ins forward called Phil Davies who had taken his first big rugby step in the opposite direction. He was born in Seven Sisters, near Neath, but joined Llanelli at the age of 19. He is a year younger than Jonathan and had played for Welsh Schools and Welsh Youth. Coincidentally, both he and Jonathan made their debuts for Wales in the same game.

A year later they again played together for Wales in a Cardiff international and in the hotel afterwards Jonathan was briefly joined by a young lady with whom he exchanged a few sharp words. Since Phil doesn't speak Welsh and wasn't introduced he was unaware that he was witnessing a normal exchange of frank views between Jonathan and his sister Caroline.

The following night Caroline turned up again. By this time their celebrations had meandered the 60 miles up from Cardiff and had come to rest at Llanelli where it was very clear that Jonathan could proceed no further. Caroline was deputed to drive him home to Cefneithin where Karen was impatiently waiting. Phil had to carry Jonathan into the car and out again at the other end.

Seven months after this unpromising meeting Phil and Caroline were married and thereafter she became the proud possessor of two Davieses in the Welsh team, one her brother, the other her husband and much confusion has arisen from it.

Jonathan and Karen had married two years earlier. It was a top hat and tails affair with a honeymoon in Tenerife. The house they had planned to live in was snatched from them when the deal fell through two days before the wedding so they moved in with Karen's mother and father. Since Jonathan was treated more as a son than a son-in-law it was by no means the problem these arrangements can be and although they were unaware of it at the time, it meant that they spent the last six months or so of her father's life in closer proximity to him than they would otherwise have done.

When they did get round to buying a house, it was a big four-bedroomed house in Cefneithin with views down the Gwendraeth valley, a bargain at £20,000. Jonathan's job and his rugby were going well, Karen was enjoying her work at the hospital – they had all the equipment for a happy and settled life.

The first intimation that a well-ordered existence might be difficult to achieve came to Karen when they went down to Tenby for a day in the summer after he got his cap.

We went to a bar for a drink, when a couple of men just came up and butted in. They were excited at seeing Jonathan and just wanted to chat but they completely cut me out of the scene. It was as if I had suddenly ceased to exist. Jonathan could see I was unhappy but he wasn't used to that sort of thing either and found it hard to get rid of them. I realised then that he wasn't just mine, he was public property.

Of course, the better he did the worse it got. It wasn't me having a fit of pique because of the adulation he was getting. I like watching him play as much as anybody does. He's great and he is obviously going to be a centre of attraction. But in Wales they treat rugby players like Jonathan as if he is their possession, as if he belongs to the nation not to himself. They expect him to do everything, be everywhere, even stop in the middle of his meal to have a chat to them in a restaurant.

It is amazing how different it is in Widnes. He is just as popular up north as he was in Wales but they are much more respectful of him as a person. They like to say hello and get his autograph but they are polite and sensible about it. We can go out and relax and be together much easier than we can at home. They like him in Widnes but they don't feel they own him.

It didn't help when Neath made him captain. Apart from the training nights, there were social and official functions he had to attend in Neath before making the 30 minute drive back to Cefnei-thin. He wouldn't be home until well past 11 p.m. and he still had his job to get off to in the morning.

The tours abroad – the 80,000 miles travelling he did in 1986 represented a long time away from Karen – the games and engagements all over the country increased as his fame and reputation increased. Each one represented another strain on the relationship.

In January 1987, when Jonathan was wowing the Neath fans with some of the best club performances of his career, they separated. It didn't last long. Within two weeks they were back together trying to heal the breach. But less than a month later they separated for what looked like forever. Jonathan moved out and took a flat in Neath and the house was sold.

Naturally, both families were horrified and Jonathan's mother, although convinced it would all turn out well in the end, was concerned how he would cope on his own. For all his confidence and maturity he had no experience of living on his own, either mentally or physically.

Whatever benefits accrue to a man from an abrupt return to bachelorhood, they soon evaporate in the stale air of an empty and uncared for home. Being based in Neath was an immediate advantage, relieving him of the long journey home and the inevitable cool reception, but it soon became a doubtful freedom. His mother began receiving frequent visits and often went to Neath to restore some comfort to his disorganised flat. The evidence of Jonathan's unsuitability and lack of genuine enthusiasm for the gadabout's life was piling up.

But it was from within that he was feeling the biggest discomfort, the distortions that glory had brought to his life were taking their toll. He is not the first, nor will he be the last, young man pushed to the brink of personal catastrophe by a rush of sporting success and the resulting adulation but, considering what can happen in these circumstances, a brief totter on the edge represents a lucky escape.

Jonathan's sister Caroline is sure that the break came at a vital time. If things had drifted on in the same way he might have gone over the edge.

'He is not the hard, arrogant so-and-so he seems to be on the field. He can do brilliant things there, but off it he is just another human being capable of making mistakes like anyone else. It is difficult to become everyone's hero without it affecting you in some way and there was a time when he didn't cope with it very well. That made it very hard for Karen.'

Caroline can well remember her feelings at the time. 'We have our words but we're very close. He is supposed to be more easy going than me, but deep down he's a worrier. He used to call at the house and knock the door and when I'd shout and ask who it was he'd reply, "Jonathan" and I would ask, "Is that Jonathan the great rugby player or Jonathan my brother?" and he would say, "Come on Caroline, stop messing about." But he got the message.'

'All of us who loved him, and obviously Karen the most, just wanted him to pause and take stock of things, to realise what was happening to him. He did and it has worked out well.'

But the happy ending wasn't all that easily achieved and the time it took for the wounds to their marriage to be fully healed was long and painful. There is no doubt that the personal blows he took to his spirit had an effect on his game. The Five Nations Championship did nothing to enhance his reputation and when the confusion over his future began to eat into his relationship with Brian Thomas, another prop to his stability was removed.

Although he was in fairly regular contact with Karen by telephone there was no firm move towards a reconciliation before it became time for him to leave for Australasia with the Welsh World Cup squad. His morale before stepping onto rugby's greatest ever stage was not what it should have been.

It is grossly unfair to suggest that Jonathan flopped in the World

Cup. Perhaps he didn't live up to expectations but that may have been because they were too high considering the standard and pressures of this first concentration of the best of world rugby. Although Wales finished a creditable third, it was not a good Welsh side and from the point of view of personal performance, Jonathan found himself overshadowed by Robert Jones, John Devereux and Paul Moriarty, justifiably in his view.

Clem Thomas, former Welsh captain and now one of the game's foremost authorities, felt that Jonathan still managed to give the impression he was a class above the other outside halves on view. 'But he never really had much of a chance to prove it, with the Welsh forwards crumbling in front of him. There were flashes of brilliance we know he has but the lack of opportunity to express himself in the way that he can, meant it was a muted campaign for him.'

Jonathan's best performance was against Canada when he was made captain in place of the injured Richard Moriarty. After an indifferent first half, Jonathan inspired Wales to a second half performance that wrecked Canada with eight tries. There was a call for Jonathan to be retained as captain for the rest of the tournament but if the Welsh selectors were tempted to give him the job, they managed to resist it.

Wales, having also beaten Ireland and Tonga in their Group matches, went on to beat England in the quarter finals but were then comprehensively defeated by the eventual winners, New Zealand, in the semis. In the match to decide third and fourth placings, Wales beat Australia 22–21. Since the Aussies were reduced to 14 men during most of the game it was held to be a dubious victory and one, furthermore, not gained until a last minute kick by Paul Thorburn.

Stephen Jones of the *Sunday Times* was another who refused to conform to the opinion that Jonathan's World Cup was a failure. He wrote, 'Davies played with insistent excellence throughout. He killed Ireland with his kicking, shredded Canada with ball in hand. He made some brilliant plays against England and even, on the day of his team's humiliation, against New Zealand. He provided one of the most breathtaking individual moments of the whole tournament with an astonishing trick drop-out and 50-yard burst against Australia.'

While all this was going on Jonathan made frequent calls home to Karen, and dared to hope that things might return to normal.

But when he returned home, if not a conquering hero then half of one, he found that Karen was packing to go on holiday to Miami.

It was irony in its sharpest form and, although it hadn't been planned that way, a master stroke psychologically. It had always been Jonathan who went away, leaving Karen feeling sad and deserted. Now Karen was stepping onto an aeroplane bound for an exotic destination and Jonathan was feeling abandoned. It was a persuasive piece of role reversal.

Reconciliation negotiations began on her return and within a couple of months they were back together where the marriage had started – in Karen's Cefneithin home with her mother Virene. By November Karen was able to announce that she was pregnant, and there we could put up the 'Happy Ever After' sign were it not for a small black cloud forming on the horizon.

While Jonathan and Karen were separated he went out with a young lady from Port Talbot and, even as the couple began to rebuild their lives together, she was telling the *Daily Mirror* all about it.

▽ J.D.

When the screaming front page headlines of one of our nastier tabloid newspapers denounced me as a 'Rugby Rat' early in 1988 I suppose I joined an elite band of royalty, cabinet ministers, film stars and pop idols who have had their reputations blackened in this way. I can't remember being flattered by being included in such company.

And if any of them actually read the details of my great 'crime' I doubt if they or any self-respecting rotter would consider I was good enough to be associated with them. My team-mates at Llanelli were very sympathetic and promptly christened me 'Roland'.

The facts are quite simple. While Karen and I were apart I took out a girl from Port Talbot. I enjoyed her company, I met her mother and father and we got on very well. But when there was a chance of being reunited with Karen, I obviously made that my priority and, thank God, we got back together.

I don't know what made the girl speak to the press or even when she did so. But it looks like they kept the story until I was in the public eye, i.e. the start of the Five Nations Championships in January, and then splashed it over the front page.

It wasn't very inspiring stuff. Just that I had finished my relationship with her to become reconciled with my wife and start a family.

There was nothing more revealing or more scandalous and for that I was labelled a 'Rugby Rat', although I suppose that was the newspaper's word rather than hers. But it wasn't as if we lived together, or that I left her at the altar or even on the steps of a maternity home.

It was all a bit tame and if I hadn't been playing for Wales at the time, I doubt if it would have been worth printing. But the headline is what people read and seeing it there was a harrowing experience. As Karen said, something that had been very personal had been made very public.

Fortunately I had told Karen about it all at the outset and the rest of the family knew. But it still was a blow, especially as we were living with Karen's mother. As ashamed as I was to bring this down on everyone I was able to get through it because of the support of those close to me. If I have been unfortunate in losing the main male influences in my life, I have been very lucky in the women who are near and dear to me. My mother's strength is matched by my sister's, Karen is someone I've proved I can't do without and her mother Virene has been absolutely tremendous. I wonder how many men could have survived living with their mother-in-law when a story like that came out!

When I look back on it now, it seems as if it happened to someone else. There's no doubt that the glory was all too much for me to take in, once I'd gained my first cap and started to get invited around the world.

I began neglecting Karen and my home, our little arguments grew and grew and we drifted apart. Then came the split and the involvement with someone else – it is a pretty familiar plot but I still regret the hurt I caused to Karen.

Slowly it dawned on me what a mess I was making of things. I had allowed the pressure and temptations of popularity to destroy my liking for the normal parts of life. It seems to put you on a high, make you look for excitement all the time. People note who my sporting heroes are and think that I was trying to live up to some high-flying image. But I never intentionally set out to do that. I just found it difficult to say 'no'.

You don't intentionally set out to do anything, you just react to being the centre of attraction. It is impossible for it not to affect you in some way.

Now I understand what makes these sporting idols go off the

rails. I came to my senses because I've got strong family and friends and because I don't think I'm cut out for that sort of life anyhow.

By the time I got to the World Cup I had realised how much I missed Karen and how stupid I'd been. Then I found the main difference between myself and my heroes – they can misbehave and still play out of their skins but I'm the opposite. There's no doubt that being away from Karen was affecting my game. I could still go through the motions, even make good moves, but that little bit extra that comes instinctively just wasn't operating as usual.

I don't have to read the press to know how I've done. And I certainly don't think I was as far off form as some of them said. But I wasn't at my best. I let myself down.

Even now I regard it as a great opportunity missed, and all through my own stupidity. The final blow came when we arrived back in Cardiff after a 27-hour journey and Karen was the only wife not waiting to greet us.

But at least something constructive came out of it. It took away all doubts about how much I loved Karen and how important she is to me. Our relationship was undoubtedly strengthened once we went back together. And I believe I am a better player and a more contented man.

Playing for Widnes brings me just as much attention as I got in Wales but I take it in my stride, spend most evenings at home and although I like a good drink with the boys after a game I try to take Karen out as often as possible. She and Scott are my chief interests now.

But this settled life is not just a reaction to our parting – there were plenty of other things at that time to make my life a misery.

As if my leaving Neath amid all that rumour wasn't difficult enough, my arrival at Llanelli was doomed to be a disappointment.

When I returned from the World Cup I was hoping to have a rest before announcing my future plans. But speculation was driving me and everyone else mad. Every day I seemed to be linked with a different club, Swansea one day, Cardiff the next. There were plenty of rumours about there being an auction, about me going to the top bidder, so I decided to announce my decision which was of course always going to be Llanelli.

I informed Neath of my decision and had that great feeling of walking into Stradey to meet their officials and sign on. Perhaps it was six years later than it should have been, but that wasn't my fault. I was at the club of my dreams and as I told them, 'I am coming to run, not to kick', which is the sort of brave thing you have to say when you are following fly-halves like Phil Bennett, Barry John, Carwyn James, Gareth Davies and the man who had 'gone north' to Hull the previous season, Gary Pearce.

I was very excited about the prospect of playing for what was my home club in first class rugby and it was great to join brother-in-law Phil at my first training session in which I ran around like a lunatic. I couldn't wait for the season to start. I didn't think twice when an invitation came to play in the Lords Taverners Sevens in London because it was just the job to sharpen me up.

Unfortunately I neglected to seek permission from Llanelli and even more unfortunately, I injured my knee and put myself out for ten weeks. A lot of people had bought season tickets for Stradey on the strength of my arrival there and they were not happy, to say the least. It brought another load of critical publicity.

I received a public ticking off in his column by Phil Bennett who said, 'Llanelli have good reason to be annoyed. Sometimes I don't think players are sufficiently considerate. They shouldn't take off to play in odd matches without having the courtesy to ask their club's permission.'

My debut finally came three months later against New Zealand club Petone which we won after a hard battle but I then hurt a hamstring and had the pleasure of being called a malingerer in the press.

But even when I did settle down to play I appeared to disappoint some people who thought I was not doing enough individually. The fact that I was trying to fit in to a different style of play and not just trying to be flashy on my own account obviously didn't occur to them.

I had been frequently criticised before for doing the things that suited me and not the team. But that isn't true. I am a fervent team man and everything I do in any game I play is directed towards helping the team to win.

I learned a couple of painful lessons from that experience. After I hurt my knee in the sevens, which just locked solid, I was carried in and dumped on the physio's table. People popped in to see if I was able to get back on the field but when it was obvious that I wouldn't be re-appearing that day, I was just ignored. One minute I was the shining light, the star attraction, and the next I was a useless lump of meat. It was an object lesson in what risks you run doing favours for people.

I was in a state trying to work out how I was going to get back to Wales when I couldn't walk. I couldn't even get my clothes on. Luckily Cliff Morgan arrived on the scene and was brilliant when he saw how distressed I was about suffering such a bad injury and worried about getting home.

He called a taxi and told the driver to take me to Cefneithin and send the bill to the Lords Taverners. The fare for the journey was £525 but I can't see how I would have got home otherwise.

The other lesson, of course, concerned my duty to Llanelli.

At the Gnoll my duties were clear, to make the most effective use of the ball won for us by our highly mobile forwards. This I did by taking the responsibility upon myself to make breaks and set things up. We didn't score 113 tries in 25 games through selfishness.

Llanelli relied on a different format. They had a great pack, yes, but they also had excellent backs, including my friend and World Cup colleague Ieaun Evans on the wing. I saw my duty as to make sure players like him saw plenty of the ball. So instead of making the number of breaks I did at Neath I often fed the centre as quickly as possible. I was thinking of the team and, in the long run, our results showed it was a policy that came off. Llanelli lost only two games.

But it was a no-win situation for me. If I used every ball myself I was accused of being selfish and too individualistic but if I spread it I was getting rid of the responsibility, ignoring my duties and failing to please the fans.

At the same time my place in the Welsh team had become the centre of most conversations. While I was off injured Wales played an international against the American Eagles and won 46–0. Playing at outside half was Bleddyn Bowen, an excellent player who often appeared at centre and whose style was different to mine.

The opinion was voiced that perhaps Wales should have a more orthodox outside-half like Bowen and less of the flamboyant solo stuff I brought to the position. It was also suggested that I would benefit from a switch to full back. This speculation sparked me to work harder.

My only consolation was that I was settling down gradually at Llanelli and at the turn of the year managed to get a chance to shine for the Baa-Baas in their annual match against Leicester. Les Cusworth, the Leicester and former England fly-half, attracted all the headlines, even though I thought I'd played a blinder which included a 70-yard run for a try. Times were obviously getting hard.

They were about to get a little harder, what with the *Daily Mirror* getting ready to explode their bombshell. But that wasn't the half of it. During one week I was hit by a hat-trick of horrors. Karen had a car smash on a Tuesday from which she emerged mercifully unscathed and with no problems with the pregnancy. Then I had an accident two days later, but was not so lucky.

I had been to the funeral of the famous little Welsh referee Gwyn Walters and afterwards, as often happens at Welsh funerals, I joined Phil May and other mourners for a drink. One led to another and instead of getting a taxi or begging a lift, I climbed into the car. I was hungry so I stopped for an Indian meal.

Some reports say I was actually eating the meal as I was driving along but this was not true. Suddenly the car skidded as I came to the outskirts of Felinfoel, shot across the road and demolished a lamp-post. I wasn't hurt but the police soon arrived and I regret to say I failed the breathalyser. I discovered later that someone tried to buy the broken lamp-post as a souvenir.

I never knew a man could get into so much trouble in the space of a year. I was assured that there was a time when Wales's outside half would have been excused anything, even murder. Perhaps they'd seen me play, because I received a two-year ban. I did get the impression that I received a long ban because I was in the public eye and they wanted to make an example but, although it was my first driving offence, nothing condones what I did and I shall never do it again.

To complete the troubles of that week, I was captain of the Probables in the final Welsh trial on the Saturday. The Possibles beat us 7–3!

11
Neath and the Noose

Anyone worried about Jonathan's ability to keep his considerable pecker up after the trials and torments of 1987 would have been heartened by his contribution in deed and word to the traditional Christmas holiday fixture played by the Barbarians at Leicester.

On Boxing Day he had jammed a gag into the mouths of his critics by scoring 24 points, including two tries, and generally masterminding Llanelli's 44–13 defeat of London Welsh. Two days later he trotted out in the famous hooped Barbarians jersey to take part in what turned out to be an excellent game in which defeat for the Baa-Baas by 48–30 did not stop him reminding everyone of the extent of his repertoire.

He scored a 40-metre drop goal to give the Baa-Baas the half-time lead and scored the try of the match when he jinked and swerved through most of the Leicester team to seal a performance which, according to one critic, 'totally eclipsed everyone else on view'. But it was Les Cusworth, Leicester's veteran outside half and inspiration of his team's victory, who was acclaimed the hero at the after-match dinner.

One speaker said he hoped that Les would be selected for England in the Five Nations Championships. 'I hope so too,' shouted Jonathan in what was an unmistakably brash declaration that he would be happy to take on Cusworth at Twickenham.

It was a welcome display of the old cockiness, especially since Jonathan was in no way sure of his own place in that confrontation. The Welsh air rang with calls for his place in the team to be reviewed in the light of the way they played without him against America and his lack of big-match practice since his return from the World Cup.

Claims and conspiracies on behalf of alternative choices are something every Welsh rugby international gets used to, especially the
outside half whose position is potentially the most glorious and thus
the most vulnerable.

The virtues of some young hotshot from another valley are circu-
lated with the same relish that once adorned tales of the latest
gunslinger in the wild west. They are just as likely to bite the dust
at the first testing examination of their credentials, but there's always
another one somewhere else.

Jonathan accepted this as part of the task of filling that red No.
10 jersey and if he needed help in coping with the pressure it came
from those who knew only too well what he was going through.

So many Welsh rugby players become writers and commentators
when they retire that the press box at the National Stadium
resembles Mount Olympus, with the gods of the past looking down
on the mortals below and passing judgement upon them.

It doesn't ease the pressure. Imagine a plumber having to work
under the scrutiny of a collection of the world's best ex-plumbers,
ready to criticise his every move.

It was significant how many of them were encouraging, particularly some of his illustrious predecessors. Barry John and Phil Bennett
rejected claims that he should be replaced and Gareth Davies, the
player so rudely shoved aside to make way for him, wrote in the
Sunday Express: 'His extreme confidence in his own ability and
disregard for opponents has obviously not been dented by injuries
and criticism. He has fought back and perhaps is now ready to
accept the responsibility of leading Wales to greater honours and
renewed success . . . '

John Taylor, the former Welsh wing forward of the triumphant
'seventies, wrote in the *Mail on Sunday* about the Welsh tradition
of putting players on a pedestal and then trying to knock them off
it at the slightest disappointment. 'Since his return from injury, he
has transformed Llanelli from an unhappy shambles into a team
with poise and purpose. He is one of the few who can do the same
for Wales. Talk of leaving him out of the national team is nonsense.'

And an eloquent plea was added by Paul Rees in the *South Wales
Echo*. 'Is it Davies's fault Wales have entered a long period of
transition? Is it his fault Wales have not been able to match several
other countries at forward, that our traditional flair has been buried
beneath the crash ball, slow movements and defensive options? Were
Jonathan Davies Australian, All Black, South African, French, Scott-

ish or Irish we would be hailing him as one of the truly greats. But he is Welsh and he is in the stocks with buckets of rubbish being pelted at him. The indictment is against us, not Davies.

'He is a flame burning in a dark hour and we seem to be trying desperately hard to blow it out. Why?'

When the team to meet England was announced Jonathan was in, not as captain as many would have liked, but certainly as outside half. But the selectors did produce a shock. Anthony Clement, the young Swansea outside half who had been promoted as main rival for Jonathan's position, was chosen as full back in place of Paul Thorburn, the finest goal-kicker in Europe.

The warning was quite clear – no-one's place was secure and since the side contained four outside halves – Jonathan, Clement, Bleddyn Bowen who had moved to centre, and Mark Ring – the point was not lost on Jonathan.

It was a situation that required an urgent rebuttal of all the slights and assertions that had been directed at him, otherwise his name might not survive another selection meeting.

As the team took their positions Jonathan's eyes roamed over the opposition ranks, seeking someone he could upset with a cheeky greeting. His gaze fell upon Les Cusworth and he remembered he had a boast to fulfil in that direction too.

What happened next is best left to him to describe in the following chapter, but Wales won 11–3 and skipper Bleddyn Bowen said: 'I was not surprised by Jonathan – we know what he is capable of. This was one of his most influential games for Wales. He had a marvellous match and showed true brilliance.'

The following international, against Scotland in Cardiff, brought him even greater praise. He scored a superb try and dropped two goals in the last eight minutes to help Wales win a close match 25–20.

One of the critics he won over was former Welsh skipper Mervyn Davies who told a reporter, 'People have been comparing him with Barry John and Phil Bennett for some time, but I couldn't see it. But on Saturday he took the game by the scruff of the neck. He was in charge, and it was a wonderful spectacle.'

Barry John himself commented, 'Jonathan Davies is now the team's inspiration and in his present mood the Triple Crown and the Grand Slam are there for the taking.'

Wales had not won the Triple Crown for nine years and not the Grand Slam for ten. To achieve both they had to beat Ireland in

Dublin and then France in Cardiff. Any optimism they felt was diluted by the memory of how often Dublin had proved to be the graveyard of Welsh hopes.

It was not to be this time. Wales won a hard and dour game 12–9, thanks to a late penalty by Paul Thorburn. It was a tough match, with tempers on edge, but Wales were determined to battle it out to win the Crown. Jonathan's contribution was the inevitable dropped goal but he missed with three attempts in the second half.

So the Grand Slam was available to be won on Welsh soil against the dominant team of the 'eighties, France. In the event, France did not play at their brilliant best. Neither did Wales, failing to take their chances in a tough match. The French won by the narrowest of margins, 10–9, and the slimmest of reasons to celebrate; they shared the championship with Wales.

But at least a Welsh side that was given little hope at the beginning of the championships had managed to produce a Triple Crown triumph in a brilliant style that was reminiscent of the glorious 'seventies.

And for Jonathan came an added sweetness: for his part in helping Wales win the Triple Crown he was chosen as Whitbread Rugby World Player of the Year. From suspect starter to Player of the Year in three matches is quite a leap forward.

There was one last hurdle before the end of the season and preparation for the Welsh tour of New Zealand in the summer. Llanelli were powering their way towards the Schweppes Welsh Cup, and steamrollering in the opposite direction to meet them were Neath who had made an excellent recovery following the loss of Jonathan and were being talked of as clear-cut favourites to win the Cup.

Anyone who saw the final as anything but a collision between Jonathan and his former mentor Brian Thomas had no eye for drama.

▽ J.D.

The card arrived the day we were playing Neath in the final of the Schweppes Welsh Cup at the National Stadium in Cardiff. I saw the postmark and thought how nice it was that someone from Neath should send me a card.

Then I opened it and saw my photograph on the front, with a noose drawn around my neck and the letters RIP written underneath. Inside there was no message, just the signatures of the entire Neath team. Perhaps it was a joke, but jokes don't make your stomach turn over and your skin shiver.

It so happens that Neath are a team who indulge in a quite original form of horseplay, with not many holds barred. I remember once falling asleep on the team coach on the way back from a match and waking up feeling a bit damp and smelling funny. I had been used as a convenience. I was able to laugh at that because that was our bit of fun and it didn't matter that I was the captain. Fair play, I managed to get my own back in various ways I won't describe here. I wouldn't like you to get the wrong idea about Neath. Horseplay and a hideous variety of practical jokes are a large part of the enjoyment of playing rugby. Neath indulge more heartily than most but I thought it was fun at the time.

But I didn't think the noose was at all funny, and what's more I didn't think it was meant to be. It was sickening and made me lose a lot of respect for certain members of the Neath club.

When I got to the ground I showed it to the other Llanelli boys and they didn't think it was funny either. They urged me to keep it, to show it to someone in the press. I just tore it up there and then. And I thought to myself – right, you bastards, there's no way you're going to win the game.

I'd played alongside most of those boys for four seasons. I worked hard, played some good rugby, shared a lot of success with them. And when I left, not entirely of my own choosing, I was sincere when I wished them all the best. And I have to admit that they'd done very well if not better without me. Not that I expected them to collapse the moment I walked out of the door, but it does take time to replace a key player and to change your style to suit the new man. At least I left when they were on the top; I had plenty of offers to leave them when they were on the bottom.

I certainly had to change my style to suit Llanelli's policy of bringing their entire back division into the action as often as possible. But when the Cup Final against Neath loomed we had to think very hard about the best way to tackle them. Their strength was still based on a strong and mobile pack and we had a taste of that power when they beat us 57–9 at the Gnoll. We didn't have a full team out but it was still a nasty reminder of how good they were.

Our coach Gareth Jenkins, whom I enjoyed working with tremendously, was convinced that our main hope of surprising Neath was to prepare our forwards both physically and organisationally to take on Neath up front. We had the players, Gareth provided the plan and the motivation, and Neath walked in to a type of opposition they didn't expect.

Brian Thomas and Ron Waldron, just like all the pundits, anticipated that the game would be a straight conflict between two differing styles – their power and speed in the pack against the pace and skill of our backs. They planned accordingly and while we announced our team well in advance Brian kept his formation secret until an hour before the kick-off.

Then he dropped a bombshell by leaving out their giant No. 8 Mark Jones in order to play three flankers in the back row and quicken their attack on me. If they could nail me regularly it would not only give them a lot of pleasure, it would cut off the supply to the Llanelli three-quarters.

But we didn't intend to play to what was regarded as our strength. We were going to play to our forwards who proceeded to produce the game of their lives. Phil May and Phil Davies were absolutely brilliant, and our front five won a share of the ball that was way beyond expectations. Our scrum half Jonathan Griffiths took the right options and when David Pickering, the Neath flanker who was due to contain me, came looking for me I just kicked for position.

It was a brilliant day. The attendance was just under 57,000 which was a new world record for a club match and every time I touched the ball the Neath fans booed and whistled like I was the villain in a pantomime. What with that and the memory of that card I had all the incentive I needed.

Anyone watching us for the first time wouldn't have thought we had any three-quarters, because every time I got the ball I kicked it. We had the advantage of a stiffish breeze in the first half and I made full use of it, getting 60 to 70 yards on my touch kicks which were all bouncing right and driving them back down the field. To keep forcing them back down the field, to avoid mistakes and to put them under continual pressure – those were our aims and they worked a treat, particularly as the absence of Mark Jones helped us win plenty of extra line-outs.

The Neath forwards got so annoyed they started giving away penalties. I scored four penalties that afternoon, each one to a chorus of boos and jeers that made them all the sweeter as they went over. I got hammered a couple of times by Phil Pugh but I expected that. We won 28–13 and even Neath had to acknowledge that we walked away with it. Then I was named Man of the Match by the biggest margin ever recorded, and I can't remember being happier.

It brought to an end my first season with Llanelli, one that had started so badly and looked at one time as if it would mark a low point in my international career. As it turned out I helped Wales win the Triple Crown, and so nearly the Grand Slam, and played in a great Llanelli team who won the Welsh Cup.

When I look back at the start of that international championship, which also coincided with the nasty story about me in the *Daily Mirror* and my drink-driving case, I believe I was still suffering from the aftermath of bad feeling about my unwise words in that magazine article a year previously. And perhaps the pressure of being called the new Messiah and all that rubbish didn't help. But I knew I was more mature as a person and a player and it would have been ironic if I had been dropped.

But I could be sure of one thing. Everything I had done before, every good match I had played, was wiped clean. I would be starting again, having to prove myself from scratch – otherwise I'd be ending up with the title of 'flash in the pan'. It wasn't only me on trial, there was a lot of talk that we were lucky in the World Cup and would soon be found out.

The opening match of the Five Nations Championship was against England at Twickenham and I was very relieved when the team was announced and my name was in its usual place at outside half. There had been a great deal of speculation that either I wouldn't be picked – and there was a faction within the WRU who would have happily seen me replaced – or I would be tried out at full back. I didn't take the proposed positional switch seriously because that would have meant dropping Paul Thorburn and I couldn't see that happening.

But happen it did, not to make room for me but for a rival outside half, Anthony Clement of Swansea who had scored two tries as substitute centre against America. Paul was thunderstruck and so was most of Wales. It was his brilliant kicking that had helped gain us third place in the World Cup with that narrowest of wins over Australia. Now he was to be thrown out to make room for a 20-year-old player who had not only never played a full game for Wales before, he'd never played full back at all.

It was a decision, the selectors explained, aimed at creating a more inventive and attacking back division, giving us more options. I had my suspicions that there was another reason. There was such a powerful lobby for Anthony to replace me, that putting him in at full back was a compromise. It was not the decision but the way it was done that lives longest in the memory. Paul had done wonders for Wales and deserved a quiet warning about their intentions, but with their typical disregard for the feelings of the players, the selectors just read out the team in a crowded dressing room. He was thunderstruck.

Certainly what happened to Paul and the fact that Anthony was obviously breathing down my neck were pointers that I couldn't ignore. My place in the Welsh team was hanging on my performance at Twickenham. It was exactly the situation I welcome – it didn't help my nervousness but it did wonders to my motivation.

In many ways it was worse for Anthony. It doesn't help when you take the place of a popular player but to play in a strange position, and one in which you can be put under tremendous pressure by high kicks, makes it twice as difficult.

But he had an excellent game. I like Anthony as a player. He has plenty of pace and is not afraid to use it and despite it being his debut he didn't put a foot wrong. The decision to play him was proved right but, on the other hand, no-one could say we didn't miss the Thorburn boot. We didn't put the ball over the posts once. There were two penalties from just inside our own half at a crucial time for us. Mark Ring missed both of them and I would have put a lot of money on Paul getting at least one. Had the game swung on those kicks, as it could so easily have done, the selectors would have been in trouble.

But Wales were able to produce two brilliant tries that won the game and reminded many people what open, creative rugby we were capable of. Don't forget that England had been unlucky to lose 10–9 to France in Paris two weeks earlier.

It was a very satisfying match for me. Some said it was the best I'd played but I find comparisons like that hard to make because each game has its own problems. But I had produced a good display when I needed to and that made it important. It might have been even more memorable for me had I scored in the first half when I looked certain to do so.

It was a fairly even first 30 minutes but I had missed two drop goal chances and I was itching for a chance to get England back on their heels. Then Mark Ring put me away on the half way line and I dummied my way into a gap and went like hell for the line. The England full back Jon Webb had bought the dummy but unknown to me had made a great recovery. I was only a couple of yards from the line when my legs were suddenly grabbed from under me and my vision of a try was replaced by a faceful of Twickenham grass.

I understand that someone in the press box shouted, 'He's not as quick as he was.' I think I might have answered that allegation since, but the remark proves that some people prefer to be negative rather than positive. It suited that person to think I was caught because I was slow, rather than Webb was quick. So let's put the record straight – it was Webb's legs that saved England, not mine.

And after the tackle one of mine was feeling decidedly dodgy around the ankle. It was strapped up at half-time but it felt none too good as we went into the second half with neither side having scored. The main thing was that I could still run on it. It was painful and forced me to hobble now and then but there was no way I was going off.

England had the wind behind them in the second half and they started as if they were going to make full use of it. My opposite number Les Cusworth was still looking to test Anthony Clement with some high kicks but one of them proved to be England's undoing. Not only did Clement catch it, he ran it straight back at them and set up a ruck from which the ball was passed to me. I brought in Ring, then Clement came into the line again, then Ring and Adrian Hadley did a magical scissors move for the winger to finish a great move with a try.

I was trying to move the ball quickly to save my ankle but midway through the second half I decided to try to open things up again. I was well in my own half and a long kick for touch was on but I thought I'd give my ankle a chance to run the ball. I found myself going on a wide loop towards the left of the England defence shaking off Mike Skinner, who'd already given me one thump. It was obviously not what they were expecting and the Welsh boys came swarming in support. I passed to Ring who cut inside and found Richie Collins with a long pass which the wing forward picked up brilliantly. He sent Bob Norster away and Bob's pass reached Bleddyn Bowen who put Hadley away for another great try.

I made it 11 points with a drop goal and Webb scored England's only three points with a late penalty. It was a splendid win but it was the manner of it that was so rewarding. I was sad for Cusworth. Things hadn't gone well for him but he was the first to come to see if I was all right after Webb's tackle. He never played for England again, but he is an excellent player and a real gentleman. I'm glad to say he's still a good friend.

There was some doubt whether my ankle, which swelled up like a balloon afterwards, would recover in time for the game against

Scotland at Cardiff but at least the doubt about my deserving a place in the team had been removed.

The ankle responded to treatment and I was fit to play in what turned out to be a magnificent and exciting game, rated one of the best ever seen at the Arms Park, and one of the most personally rewarding of any I've played in.

Alan Tait, now my good friend and team-mate at Widnes, who played in the centre for Scotland that day, never ceases to remind me how close they came to beating us – and I have to agree that for long periods they looked like doing just that. But I had the good fortune to score a try and then, in the last eight minutes, I dropped two goals that won the match; I have to keep reminding him of that.

Scotland had taken the lead after only a minute and a half with a try from Finlay Calder that Alan helped to set up. Then Gavin Hastings scored a penalty to give them a 7–0 lead. We had a couple of forays down the left but their defence was looking very sturdy.

Then came one of those moments when a flash of instinct guided me to one of my favourite tries, not least because we badly needed it. And it proved one of my theories, that there's good ball and bad ball but very often bad ball can be much better for the adventurous player.

Every stand-off likes the ball that comes whizzing into his arms as he comes running onto it. But even as he takes it the opposition are moving into position to cut down his options, so good ball for you is also red alert for them.

But a bad pass, one that you have to pick up off your toes or pull out of the air, creates that moment of doubt about your next move not only in your mind but in theirs too. And a moment of doubt in an opponent's mind is the best ally you can have.

The try I scored against Scotland was unusual enough to get it played over and over again on television and people have repeatedly asked me why I did what I did. The answer, which I'm sure they find unsatisfactory, is that the pass was so bad it confused Scotland more than it did me.

What happened was that we had a scrum about 18 yards from their line and just a few yards in from the touchline. We won the scrum but the ball squirted out unkindly for Robert Jones. He had to move sideways and backwards to reach the ball and, with the Scottish scrum half Roy Laidlaw almost on him, he flicked the ball high in my direction. Since he had his back to me at the time it was a great piece of work.

It was a stand-off's nightmare; standing flat-footed, waiting for a dropping ball, while Finlay Calder was coming at me from one direction and their outside half Andrew Ker from another. Had Robert's pass been as straight and fast as usual, Finlay would still be coming at me like a bull because he is one of the quickest breaking wing forwards in Britain and even though I would have had more time he would have been sizing me up, deciding what I was going to do next and flinging himself to stop me. But because it was a bad ball there was a new option that he didn't consider. I didn't consider it either, I just did it.

I took the ball and ran back the way it had come, side-stepping Finlay and kicking the ball low between him and the scrum which was just starting to break up. There was a channel barely a yard wide stretching between me and the line and the ball went through it like a bullet with me in pursuit.

Derek White, their big No. 8, was the only one who could turn and chase after the ball. He had a few yards start on me but I was already moving at full pace and I went past him on the line to pounce on the ball and score. I hope Derek realised I was joking after when I said if I couldn't catch someone as slow as him I would pack the game in.

The whole movement from catching the ball to scoring was pure instinct. Had I paused for even a split second either Finlay would have flattened me or the gap just wouldn't have been there. That's what I mean about a bad ball being a good one, because Scotland were thrown by it more than I was.

Things don't often fall into place like that, even for creatures of instinct like me. Anyway, my try was soon followed by a try of sheer genius by Ieaun Evans that was totally different because he didn't have the benefit of surprise. He just had the ball in his hand and four defenders between him and the line, and he just side-stepped them one after another in one of the finest runs I've seen.

That made the score 10–7 but not for long. Finlay Calder made a great break to create an attack that had Alan Tait sending over Duncan for a try. Then Gavin Hastings banged over two penalties to put them into a 17–10 lead. Early in the second half he scored a monster penalty to make it 20–10 and suddenly there seemed an awful lot to do. We just had to keep running the ball and there were some super passing movements as we flung attack after attack at them.

Then our hooker Ian Watkins scored a try which Thorburn converted. Soon after, Paul got a penalty to make it 20–19 to them. There were eight minutes left and we needed one score to take the lead, but two to be sure of winning.

There was a line-out on their twenty-five and I said to our captain Bleddyn Bowen that I was going to try a drop if it was on. He told me to go ahead. Bob Norster tapped the throw-in down and Robert sent me a beautiful pass. I could see the blue shirts coming but I took my time and sent the drop kick straight at the posts. That it was straight was about the only thing you could say in its favour. It stayed low and for an awful moment I thought it didn't have the legs to get there. But it staggered over to give us a 22–20 lead.

The Arms Park went potty but Scotland were not inclined to think the match was over. However, we drove them downfield again and won another line-out in about the same position. Bob Norster again jumped higher than anyone else but this time the ball did not come out cleanly. My Llanelli colleague Phil May helped it on its way and Robert had to bend low to scoop it and send it out to me. This time it was more of a rush and Jeffrey was almost on me before the ball left my foot but it was a much better kick, climbing high between the posts. With just a minute left that was the clincher and a great game, so fast you had to look at the video several times over to catch up with everything that happened, ended in our favour by 25–20.

I felt sorry for Scotland. They were the best team we met in the championships yet they lost narrowly to us, were beaten 22–18 in Dublin, went down 9–6 to England and yet beat France 23–12, the only British team to beat them.

We then went to Dublin to win the Triple Crown, which we did by beating Ireland 12–9 with a penalty by Thorburn three minutes into injury time. It was, we knew, not a very inspiring game. We were too busy celebrating to worry about that for a few days but after a while we began to wonder what was required of us.

At the start of the Championship we weren't given a chance of winning anything. Then we went to Twickenham and won with the best two tries seen there for a decade. We beat Scotland in Cardiff with one of the finest Welsh displays ever and then we are required to go to Ireland and fetch back the Triple Crown and produce more of the magic that two games earlier they didn't think we were capable of but now expect as a matter of course.

There are times when being an amateur rugby player means more than just not getting paid for something you devote most of your time to, it means having to satisfy the ambitions, the cravings and the egos of an entire nation. The duty involved in playing for your country can often outweigh the honour.

Going to Ireland to win any game is always a difficult quest. To go there to win a Crown or a Championship – and on this occasion they were still in with a chance of the Triple Crown themselves – is like going to take out the back teeth of a lion.

It was a delight to take part in the matches against England and Scotland, but against Ireland it was a hard, unforgiving struggle that wasn't won until the third minute of injury time. We won the Triple Crown because we deserved it and we deserved it because we played two of the three matches away from home and most of all, because we played the last one in Dublin. To look down your nose at the performance because it didn't sparkle is to dismiss the whole-hearted effort and courage of the Welsh team and of the team that sought so valiantly to stop them.

It was mainly our attitude that was at fault. Because none of us had won a Triple Crown before we allowed the pressure to build up into a fear of losing. A bit of experience in such situations would have persuaded us to stick to our strengths, to spin the ball out and use the talent we had in the backs to win comfortably.

We gained a major share of the ball to allow us to do that but we froze. We kicked away good possession and I certainly tried too many drop goals.

Looking back on matches like that I see this lack of awareness about ourselves as a team to have been a serious flaw considering the time we spent at squad sessions. The trouble is that those sessions are not used to foster teamwork and understanding. They are no more than fitness sessions. To gather the best talent from all parts of South Wales to do sprints and weights is a tremendous waste. If we are not fit at that stage of the season we never will be. That valuable time should be spent in planning for the specific challenge ahead of us. It really is an amateur approach to do otherwise.

The story of the game is simple. I scored an early drop goal. Kingston charged down an attempted touch kick by Robert Jones to score a try which made the score 6–3 to Ireland. I was then penalised for a high tackle which I swear was just around the shoulders and that made it 9–3. Paul Moriarty got a try to make it 9–9 and we battled ourselves senseless trying to force another try over their line. I missed two drop goal attempts, one drifted wide and the other was charged down, and then we were awarded a penalty that was likely to be almost the last kick of the match.

It wasn't an easy kick. On the left, about 35 yards out and a swirling breeze to contend with. I can only imagine what was going through Paul's mind. There are many moments of high pressure in sport. A snooker player, or a golfer or tennis player can face a shot that could mean the difference between winning a £90,000 first prize, or £60,000 for coming second. But Paul wasn't about to lose a penny either way. All he was kicking for was an entry in Welsh rugby history which would read either that Wales won the Triple Crown in 1988 or that Paul Thorburn lost it by missing a kick in Dublin. He wasn't even picked for the first match, and now everything depended on him.

There was irony in the air as well as a breeze when he stepped up and kicked the ball high and true between the posts. I literally jumped for joy. Another of my dreams had come true.

That we should complete the Grand Slam by beating France two weeks later at Cardiff was probably asking too much. But looking back at it now, the fact that we lost a tight game by 10–9 seems even more agonisingly close. A draw would have given us the Championship, and that was probably the least we deserved, but the Grand Slam would have been tremendous.

The disappointment was bad enough at the time. We hadn't beaten them for five years but we were all very confident. To be truthful neither of us played to our potential but they at least made the most of their chances. And, after all, to win the Crown and share the Championship was something we could console ourselves with at the time.

I think the weather had more to do with spoiling the game than any other factor. It had been dry during the week and everyone was confidently expecting a handling game – with both teams throwing it around. But it poured down on the day of the match and handling became a risky business. There was too much at stake for many risks to be taken and this thought obviously went through the minds of both teams.

I certainly felt it was a day best suited to up-and-unders. If the great French full back Serge Blanco has a weakness it is dealing with a ball dropping from a great height, especially if it is slippery and if he has to turn to take it.

It was a tactic that frequently led us to within a few yards of the French line but they kept us out, desperately at times. Had we made a breakthrough then, when the score stood at 3–3, I am sure we would have won. I might have helped by scoring a drop goal but a French hand managed to deflect the ball off its flight path.

Something was needed to break the deadlock and I felt cheeky enough to try one of my shock moves. We had a drop-out from our twenty-five and I shaped to put the customary kick into the air for the forwards to fight over. But instead of kicking it out to the left where they were all waiting, I flicked the ball downfield with the outside of my foot. I hared after it and hacked it another 30 yards. Surprise was certainly on my side because I was up to the half-way line before a Frenchman came near the ball. I gave it another whack and managed to get to their twenty-five before everybody else caught up. The situation did look promising for a couple of minutes but they beat us back. Then Lafond hit another penalty to put us 6–3 down. A period of French pressure then gave their outside half Lescarboura a chance for a try and although I was one of three Welshmen hanging on to him he just managed to crawl over the line and plant the ball down.

That made it 10–3 and although Ieaun Evans got a try which Paul converted, the score stayed at that agonising 10–9. The failure to win the Grand Slam would have been unbearable had I realised that was to be not only my last chance of appearing in the Grand Slam side but also my last Championship match. Perhaps deep down I knew, because when the whistle went I happened to have the ball in my hand and I thought I'd keep it as a souvenir.

I was making my miserable way up the tunnel still holding the ball when I felt an arm across my shoulder. I looked up straight into the eyes of Daniel Dubroca, the French captain and hooker. He nodded at the ball. Suddenly I remembered it was his last game for France whom he had captained 25 times. He is the only man ever to captain a team to three consecutive Five Nations Championships. I held out the ball and he took it with a smiling 'merci'. I wish I'd kept the bloody thing now, to mark the end of my own Five Nations career.

12

Wails within Wales

The tour of New Zealand in the summer of 1988 was probably the lowest point reached by Welsh rugby in the whole of its proud history. Those were the words used by Clem Thomas of *The Observer* and they differed only in the variety of invective from the sentiments of every writer, commentator and eye-witness of the debacle. It was unanimous – Wales stank the place out.

But Jonathan came back home smiling. Not too broadly, maybe, but enough to signify a spirit that had been uplifted by the experience rather than shattered by it. It would have been far easier had he adopted the same vacant, shell-shocked look as the rest of the nation as they contemplated two Test match defeats by the All Blacks by the total margin of a devastating 106 points to 12. But he saw only lessons to be learned and benefits to be gained from their comprehensive clattering. It was not a view that endeared him to the WRU who appeared convinced that the disgrace was nothing that a few sackings wouldn't put right. They might have even considered making Jonathan one of the scapegoats, after all he was captain for the second and final Test which Wales lost 54–9.

However, that would have been difficult because Jonathan achieved the impossible in that match. He managed to lead Wales to one of their biggest international defeats and be the game's hero at the same time. At least, he was a hero in New Zealand and one of his most treasured momentoes is a watch presented to him by Auckland supporters for being the Man of the Match.

Wales had travelled to New Zealand under the same captaincy that had led them to the Triple Crown and a share of the Championship – Bleddyn Bowen, with Bob Norster as pack leader and vice-

133

captain – and quickly discovered what a bad decision it had been to take on the tour in the first place. This should have been evident from Wales's 49–6 thrashing by the All Blacks in the semi-final of the World Cup the previous year.

In addition to being a suicide mission for the reputations newly made in the Five Nations Championship, the itinerary for the tour had been slung together in a totally amateurish and ill-informed manner. Instead of starting up the tour with easier matches to allow the squad to acclimatise before the first Test, the itinerary flung them against the toughest provincial teams.

They were already reeling before they met the full might of the All Blacks Test team at Christchurch. The result was a demoralising 52–3 defeat.

By the time the second Test in Eden Park loomed, injury as well as humiliation had taken its toll. Both Bowen and Norster were injured and Jonathan was made captain. It was like being handed control of the *Titanic*. But Jonathan had been skipper in a few of the provincial matches and had added the odd success to the tour. He scored a late drop goal to gain a 15–13 victory against Otago and scored 21 points, including two tries, in the 45–18 win over Hawkes Bay.

But he saved his best and bravest display for the second Test which saw Wales pull some dignity out of the wreckage. That they lost 54–9 hardly suggests a restoration of Welsh pride but even the All Blacks admitted afterwards that it was more like the Wales of old, that the score bore no relation to the quality of the struggle.

As for Jonathan, a great solo try near the end of the match was merely the embellishment of a courageous performance in which he tackled like a demon.

Ray Gravell, the former Wales and British Lions centre, comes from near Trimsaran and remembers Jonathan's father bringing a boy across to watch him at Llanelli. 'I remember presenting prizes at Trimsaran school when Jonathan was little more than a toddler. And that's probably how I always thought of him until that game at Eden Park. Then I saw the boy had become a man.'

Ray, who is now a popular broadcaster for BBC Wales, was perched high on the roof of the stand to do his commentary and witnessed a sight that still thrills him to talk about.

There was no way Wales could win that match. There was no way they could avoid a massive defeat, they were so heavily outgunned.

But Jonathan led them out there to give every last ounce of effort, and he was determined to lead by example. It was like Rourke's Drift, only with All Blacks instead of Zulus, which is probably worse.

He showed everything I admire in a sportsman. It is not often you get so much skill and bravery in one body. He proved he is world class that day. He was tackling men he had no business to tackle, the big back row men Shelford, Jones and Whetton didn't frighten him at all.

There were other professional witnesses eager to join the acclaim. Robert Cole of the *Western Mail* told his readers: 'It was a day on which Wales salvaged some pride and brought the Eden Park crowd to its feet with the best try of the tour. It came four minutes from the end and, fittingly enough, fell to Welsh skipper Jonathan Davies. If anyone deserved a score it was him because the work he got through in defence was remarkable. He tackled, got up and tackled again and led by example.'

Barry Newcome wrote in the *Sunday Express*: 'Not even another humiliating defeat for Wales should cloud the fact that Jonathan Davies, physically and mentally, is the man to lead their revival. This mauling was predictable but Davies, in his first major Test as captain, gave a display of commitment, bravery and skill which proved that the Welsh cause is far from lost.'

The try that brought Jonathan a standing ovation came after Mark Ring had won the ball at a ruck under the Welsh posts and ran it out before passing to Jonathan who gave it to Mason who returned it on the Welsh ten-yard line leaving Jonathan with a 60-yard run to the All Black line.

He went at it with a lunging surge that took him clear of all his pursuers apart from winger Terry Wright who wasn't able to catch Davies but flung himself in a despairing dive that enabled him to clip the Welshman's heels. Jonathan stumbled but his impetus carried him to the line for a try that made very welcome watching back home in Wales.

It was in a dingy interview room under the Eden Park stands that Jonathan added an impressive extra dimension to his performance. Instead of bemoaning their fate or complaining how distorted the score had been because Grant Fox had put over an amazing ten kicks from all parts of the pitch, he took an honest and positive view of what had happened to him and his team.

Stephen Jones of the *Sunday Times* reckoned it was almost as impressive as his courage on the field.

He had tackled the All Blacks and now he was ready to tackle the problems confronting Wales. He saw the defeats as a revelation and he knew what was needed to bring Welsh rugby up to that standard. He wanted to tell the Welsh Rugby Union's AGM all about it when they got home.

It wasn't arrogance talking. It was a young man who had shared in a bitter, almost degrading, series of defeats yet was excited by the possibilities for improvement that had been opened up. There had been so little rational analysis in the Welsh party of what they were up against. They were being outclassed and out-thought and yet they just kept plodding along without reacting or responding. He was the only one prepared to face the facts, as unpalatable as they were.

The point is that he knows the game inside out. He has a magnificent tactical brain and is not afraid to use it. I'd talked with him a lot during the World Cup the previous year and was impressed then by his grasp of the game. I think he knew what was coming and yet he walked into that New Zealand tour with his head high – and that's how he walked out of it. He was so clearly the man to lead and inspire Wales to better days.

▽ J.D.

I couldn't have been treated with more contempt if I'd suggested digging up the National Stadium and planting potatoes. My request to be allowed to address the Annual General Meeting of the Welsh Rugby Union on the subject of what to do about being wrecked in New Zealand, where we were laughed at and called the worst major touring team ever to visit there, was dismissed out of hand. At least, that's what I must assume because I didn't get the courtesy of a reply.

I hadn't been looking forward to standing up before that lot and telling them what was wrong with our game but I was prepared to if it meant we could all work towards an improvement. It wasn't as if I was a lone voice, either. Bleddyn Bowen, the original captain, had returned early because he was injured but Bob Norster, the vice-captain, stayed on, although he also became injured. And Bob was very keen to prepare a report along with other senior players. He wanted the players' point of view put forward in the hope it would help frame a new policy. They might have thought I was a cheeky upstart but Bob was one of the best and most experienced players in the world. Yet his offer fell on deaf ears as well. All we wanted was to save future Welsh teams going through what we'd been through. It was too late for us but our successors could be saved the ordeal.

I really couldn't understand their attitude. After all it was the players who suffered the real humiliation. The administrators back home were no doubt hurt and demoralised by our failure but how could they possibly not want a firsthand account from the men who came face to face with a superior rugby force and perhaps saw how we could do better next time?

They didn't even ask the coaches Tony Gray and Derek Quinnell for their frank opinions. That was because they probably intended to sack them at the first opportunity, thus following an old Welsh rugby tradition of avoiding criticism by sacking someone. The WRU cannot face problems, they just seem to wilt under public criticism and look for the nearest scapegoat.

I still think it was a disgraceful act. The best coaches that have ever been would not have stopped the All Blacks destroying us. Tony and Derek had helped us win the Triple Crown a few months earlier – now they were sacrificed.

The night before the last Test I had a meal with Gerald Davies, the great Welsh winger and now a distinguished commentator and writer on the game. We discussed the overwhelming odds facing Wales the following day and he recalled being in exactly the same position almost 20 years earlier in Wales's 1969 tour. We had lost heavily then, too, and the lessons were there to be learned. Gloomily we agreed that little progress had been attempted let alone made in the interim.

It is a tragedy that a man of Gerald's stature is not involved in the top ranks of the WRU. He, and other ex-players who occupy the press box like Clem Thomas, Barry John, Gareth Edwards and Phil Bennett, have the experience of playing and the knowledge of the game to give immense service to the Welsh game. If their voices are ignored I had a fat chance of being listened to.

When the AGM came around in June, the tour manager Rod Morgan gave his report but although Rod did his best, and correctly criticised the hotel and travel arrangements, as a leading member of the WRU he was hardly in a position to recommend the drastic measures that were needed. Rod was a genuine and much respected man and I was saddened by his death in April 1988. The thankless responsibility he had in trying to justify what happened out there would have been greatly lightened had we all, management, coaches and players, shared the burden of giving the nation a few home truths.

Ironically, not long after Rod died, the WRU announced it was appointing a committee to study the restyling of rugby administration in Wales and that one of the measures they would look at was that players should be represented on the WRU. So my idea was not so outrageous after all.

But that committee would have had a great deal more impetus had it been set up a year earlier, when that disgrace was more sharply etched in our minds. The business that Rod raised about the itinerary and the hotels will, I hope, arise again. The New Zealanders knew we were in for trouble when they saw how our fixtures had been arranged, with all the tough matches at the start. And some of the hotels were less than comfortable. In Otago some of the boys wore their tracksuits to bed because it was so cold.

But those are the joys of touring. What really upset us was that we and the All Blacks seemed to be operating under a completely different set of rules.

For a start, their liberal attitude to players earning money on the side were astonishing when compared to the slavish rules we employ in Britain. You could hardly turn a television set on without seeing an All Black endorsing this or that product. John Kirwan's book was being promoted widely – yet for us to write a book would be the end of our union days, as it was for players like Barry John and Gareth Edwards.

Most of our heroes are lost to the game because of some minor matter like that. But famous ex-All Blacks like Sid Going, Frank Oliver and Wayne Smith have a very high profile and their heavy involvement in the game is a tremendous encouragement to youngsters. Their former World Cup captain Andy Dalton is paid by a sponsor to coach counties and he is just one professional coach whose involvement I heard about.

Welsh players weren't that inferior in terms of natural skill but when it came to physical strength, fitness, freshness and appetite the All Blacks were streets ahead. Then you discover that they all have daily fitness schedules that they are sponsored to maintain. While we have to find kindly employers from whom we have to beg leave from work to train and play they get recompensed for the more frequent rugby work they do. We weren't jealous – we just wanted the same opportunities.

And when they heard how many games we play in a season the

All Blacks could hardly believe it. Our clubs play anything between 45 to 55 matches and a top player would be required to appear in between 30 and 45 of those. This compares with the 18 to 22 games an All Black is likely to feature in. How can quality flourish equally between those two different approaches?

It is hardly any wonder that they overpower us. We're probably an even match for them when we jump out of the cradle but it is a losing battle after that.

It is often said that they are much more dedicated and determined than we are. I am not surprised at that. Nor am I surprised that no top All Black ever accepts the constant stream of rugby league offers that pour across from Australia. I don't blame them. Had I enjoyed the freedoms they have I doubt if I would have been persuaded to move to Widnes.

Everything is done to make life easier for New Zealand players who represent their country. They even have a players' liaison committee who co-ordinate with the NZRU. It is made up of the captain, two other players and the immediate past captain and they discuss such matters as outfitting the team, itineraries and the involvement of wives, whose expenses to travel to Test matches are paid. Compare that with the lack of communication between the WRU and the players they appear to pick and drop as if they were toy soldiers.

How can things differ so greatly between countries that are supposed to be under the same International Rugby Board umbrella? That's what the WRU should have concentrated on when they came to evaluate the reasons for our flop.

None of what I say about New Zealand rugby is based on envy. It is pure admiration. I like the people, I like their attitudes and I love the way they play rugby. From the top administrator to the youngest player they all seem to be on the same wavelength. There's no 'them and us' divisions like there are in Wales. And whereas they don't pay their men for playing they pull out every stop to ensure they lead comfortable lives, have the benefit of any commercial or promotional activity that surrounds the game and have every encouragement and support to work on their fitness and skill levels every day.

The gap between us was so great that I believe we should have had more credit for the way we regained some dignity from the final Test. We had two new caps in the team – Jonathan Griffiths, my scrum half partner from Llanelli, and Kevin Moseley the Pontypool

139

second row – and although morale was pretty shaky we at least went out determined to give it all we had.

It is difficult to get motivated when you know you are up against stronger men who get about the park so quickly and hit the rucks like tanks, but we had no option but to tackle our hearts out.

The New Zealand skipper Wayne Shelford said afterwards that if we had played all the games like we did in the first 20 minutes they would have had a hard time beating us. But the game just ran away from us. Grant Fox was kicking goals from everywhere – the best kicking display I've ever seen – and there is nothing that saps a team's strength more than the sight of points going up on the scoreboard alongside the name of the opposing team. In my speech at the banquet afterwards I acknowledged his achievement but didn't thank him for it. I felt that if I didn't lead the way in tackling, I couldn't expect the rest of the boys to follow. I had never done so much tackling in my life, and I mean forwards as well as backs. And the late try I scored was a consolation but, even now, it is painful to look at that 54–9 scoreline.

I prefer to remember getting a standing ovation while I walked back to our half after scoring that try and one of my proudest possessions is the watch I was given as Man of the Match. Certainly the finest compliment I have ever been paid was to be told I would have made an All Black.

It was all very flattering and in some ways made up for the fact that those who run rugby in my own country didn't seem to think I was worth listening to.

How different it all might have been if that senseless tour had not been undertaken. We were wrong to go there and when you analyse what it cost Welsh rugby it may go down in history as the most stupid decision the WRU have ever made.

We were on a high in the spring of 1988. We had won the Triple Crown and shared the championship with France. We had a settled side, full of the confidence that comes from success.

What Wales should have done then was to tour a country like Canada, the USA or Japan – somewhere where we could have further jelled together, built up the team spirit that was promisingly high and worked on the understanding that was developing between our coaches, the captain Bleddyn Bowen and the players.

Then we'd have returned to face Western Samoa and Romania in good physical and mental shape. The way the Five Nations Championship turned out, a confident and settled Welsh side could have won the Triple Crown again. I would most probably have turned down a move north, we would have had a much bigger representation in the Lions squad and we would have been in great condition to play host to the All Blacks in the autumn of 1989.

I don't think all that is being too fanciful. It could have happened, and my life and the life of so many could have been vastly different.

But look what happened instead – a complete and utter shambles. Bleddyn Bowen and I talked about it when we got to New Zealand and realised what a suicide mission it was. All the hard work we'd done had come to nothing and was going to be smashed to smithereens.

The great team of the 'seventies never had to face a test like that at a vital stage of their development. They didn't tour anywhere difficult and when they did face the All Blacks, they faced them at home.

They didn't suffer the upheaval that was to follow the New Zealand humiliation. For a start the two coaches, Tony Gray and Derek Quinnell, were sent packing along with all the experience they had gained. The new coaches came in apparently determined to replace the players who had failed in New Zealand – regardless whether the replacements were any better.

Adrian Hadley had already gone north, to be followed by me and Paul Moriarty as a direct result of the New Zealand aftermath. Bleddyn Bowen, the Triple Crown captain, was treated appallingly and was driven from the scene. Richie Collins and Phil May have gone and Wales had its lowest ever representation in a Lions squad.

As a direct result of that ill-fated tour of New Zealand, Wales had deteriorated from joint European champions to a sad mess, without a sign that the WRU were learning any lessons from the experience.

13

'Cap'n Calamity'

Welsh rugby didn't lose Jonathan Davies, it threw him away. During his last six months as a union player the patriot's hawsers that bind a Welshman to his country and his game were slowly and systematically sawn through. He was then catapulted into the sympathetic arms of the Widnes coach Doug Laughton who had watched the whole process scarcely believing his luck.

As persuasive as Laughton is, his coup would not have been possible without the wholehearted, if unwitting, cooperation of the WRU.

Some say that Jonathan was always going to go to league when the time and price was right. I am not sure about that and neither is he. There's no doubt he was very tempted by the idea and he made no secret of that fact, an openness that was in no way helpful to him. But most people have a vision of something they'd like to do – such as running a country pub or sailing around the world – and never actually get around to taking a decisive step towards doing it. A timely push is what is needed.

A push certainly arrived at Jonathan's back when the time seemed exactly right – on his return from New Zealand when his dream of a new future for Welsh rugby was rudely squashed when his offer to give the WRU the player's-eye view of the lessons of New Zealand was ignored.

While he was reflecting ruefully on that he had a call from St Helens Rugby League Club, asking if he was interested in a chat. Jonathan agreed to meet the Saints chairman Joe Pickavance at Aberystwyth where Jonathan's employers, Stirling, have their head office. They talked in general terms about money and length of contract and agreed to think about it.

On July 19 Jonathan and his solicitor Malcolm Struel travelled up to St Helens and met Pickavance at his home where the offer and other contract details were presented. It was a good offer and he asked for time to think.

As Scott was born a day later it was not the best time to think over a move of this magnitude but the truth was he was reluctant to take the plunge. During his agonising we met for lunch at the Diplomat Hotel in Felinfoel and although the size and scope of the contract was mentioned it was by no means at the centre of his deliberations.

Despite his rebuff from the WRU he was still stimulated rather than demoralised by what had befallen Wales in New Zealand and said that what he wanted most from rugby at that time was not money. He wanted Wales to get back on an even keel for the Five Nations Championship, he wanted to go with the British Lions to Australia the following summer, preferably as captain, and when the All Blacks visited Wales in October 1989 he wanted to assist Llanelli maintain their great record against New Zealand tourists and lead a Welsh team good enough to avenge the humiliations of the tour just past.

If he wanted to go north after that little lot he would still be short of his 27th birthday. But, who knew, by that time rugby union might well have relaxed their rules regarding peripheral earnings. 'If it wasn't for obtaining greater security for his family, a player like me wouldn't even consider changing codes,' he said.

When St Helens rang up to see if he'd made his decision he told them of his plans. He agreed they could contact him after the Lions tour to see how he was feeling then.

He was sure he had done the right thing and faced the new season with an enthusiasm well demonstrated in the pre-season Snelling Sevens when he helped Llanelli to win the title, scoring 46 points and being declared the Man of the Tournament.

But if he saw that as a portent of a happy and successful season he was to be soon disappointed. He was about to enter the least spectacular and most perplexing period of his career. He was not beset with the troubles of 1987 but neither was he blessed with the brilliant performances that punctuated those problems.

After the triumphs of the Triple Crown and the Schweppes Welsh Cup and the tumult and tears of the New Zealand tour, perhaps it was difficult to adjust to the less demanding stresses of club rugby. There was reason for him to pick his matches, because Wales had internationals against Western Samoa in November and Romania in December, with a Barbarians game against Australia in between, but there is no doubt that his game was to suffer from the lack of testing rugby.

Llanelli's coach Gareth Jenkins said, 'He got out of the habit of making the tactical choices he used to do instinctively.'

Wales won their game against Western Samoa by an unconvincing margin compared with the sweeping victory achieved over the plucky Samoans by Ireland the previous month. But Wales were not the first international team, in rugby or soccer, to discover that smaller countries once regarded as novices in world terms were closing the gap at a rapid rate.

This truth was to be brought home in a far more devastating way a month later when Wales played Romania. Before that the Arms Park was packed for a much more glittering occasion, the Barbarians against the Australians who had been touring England and Scotland.

The Aussies won 40–22 but it was an excellent match in which Jonathan played well enough, setting up a great pitch-length move for Colin Laity. But the uncoordinated talents of the Baa-Baas were no match for the tourists in whose regimented ranks winger David Campese was on top of his brilliant form. The world record try-scorer in Tests scored two exceptional tries, the second from a weaving run past four opponents one of whom was Jonathan who did well to get a hand to Campese's waist as he side-stepped through.

Campese spends the Australian close season playing in Italy where, he told Jonathan, up to £30,000 can be earned from some clubs. The thought of spending some future winter in Italy followed perhaps by a summer in Australian rugby put the league even further from Jonathan's thoughts.

Following the disappointment of the display against the Samoans, Jonathan was expecting some discussion about the tactical approach against Romania. He had been fairly happy with his own perform-ance and had scored a good try but it had been an awkward game and one of those no-win situations; a big win would have been dismissed as easy and a narrow win as a calamity. But there certainly was a good case for a reappraisal.

All there was were several changes, including the dropping of poor Paul Thorburn for Tony Clement, which indicated the usual Welsh remedy of changing the faces not the formula. Neither was

Two great influences on my career – Brian Thomas of Neath (*below*) and Doug Laughton of Widnes

Below: Finding my first gap in rugby league – the photographers close in on my way to the bench for the Salford match

Left: Spot the newcomer! Richard Eyres kindly tells me where to go after I had come on as substitute for my debut against Salford on 15 January 1989

Right: I'm about to kick a conversion near the end of Widnes's Championship decider against Wigan. It is the hardest rugby match I have ever played in, although you wouldn't guess that by looking at me!

Below: You can't get away from New Zealanders, even with the referee's assistance. Shane Cooper of St Helens helps me to keep my chin up during a difficult period of adjustment

Widnes's rugby union 'converts'. On my left is Martin Offiah, next to him is Paul Moriarty and then Emosi Koloto. On my right is Alan Tait but he is obliterated by the bulk of Richie Eyres

The triumphant Widnes team, Championship and Premiership winners in 1989. Back row (left to right): D. Hulme, D. Smith, D. Wright, A. Currier, M. Offiah, C. Ashurst, J. Davies. Middle row: D. Pyke, E. Koloto, J. Grima, P. Moriarty, M. O'Neill, R. Eyres, D. Marsh, T. Myler. Front row: A. Tait, P. Hulme, A. Sullivan, P. McKenzie, K.Sorensen (capt), D. Myers, B. Dowd, R. Thackray

Jonathan happy about the selection of forwards for the type of game they should have been planning. He would have preferred to see a bigger pack picked.

And he was upset by a farcical incident in the week of the match. Mike Hall, the Cambridge University and Bridgend centre, had been selected for the squad but replaced because, not unnaturally, he wanted to play in the Varsity match on the Tuesday. Then Mark Ring, the splendid Cardiff centre, was dropped for turning up late for a Welsh training session. Bleddyn Bowen as the other centre in the squad appeared to be the obvious choice to replace him but the selectors instead sent for Hall. Having decided he shouldn't play because he elected to play for Cambridge they then picked him instead of Bowen who had captained Wales to the Triple Crown only eight months earlier.

Jonathan found the whole affair very puzzling and unsettling and he was very sympathetic for Bleddyn who had looked considerably bewildered and belittled when he heard the news.

There was more humiliation on the way as Wales stumbled from error to error against a Romanian team who had come equipped to spoil and contain, and certainly not to pass the ball about. It was a day when nothing was going to go right for Wales. Jonathan hit the post with an early penalty and then made the most exciting break of the game only for it to fizzle out five yards from the line for lack of support. The Arms Park echoed with the restlessness of a 17,000 crowd, barely enough to give the famous stadium any atmosphere, as Wales struggled to impose themselves.

While Jonathan tried unsuccessfully to guide and motivate his forces into commanding positions his opposite number in the Romanian team, Gelu Ignat, concentrated on winning territory with tremendous 60 and 70 yards touch kicks that constantly drove the Welsh back.

Romania won 15–9. They had given France a scare in Bucharest two weeks before, losing only 16–12, but this was their finest hour. 'The most important moment in our rugby history,' said their coach.

The Welsh inquests reached a pitch bordering on hysteria and although the criticism was general at first it soon concentrated on Jonathan and his handling of the captaincy. He had been given no pre-match instructions, no hint of how the men who had picked the team visualised it should play.

Jonathan had been the first to admit that he hadn't played well but it slowly dawned on him that the whole weight of the burden

145

was being nudged his way. The coach John Ryan spoke abstractly about lack of judgement behind the scrum but John Dawes the WRU's coaching organiser was quoted as putting the blame squarely on Jonathan's shoulders.

When I spoke to him he was questioning whether he should resign as captain. I counselled against doing something that would be seen as an admission that he considered it was all his fault, when it blatantly wasn't. 'Perhaps I'm a better player without that responsibility,' he argued. I said it was the greatest honour his country could give him. If they wanted to take it from him, fair enough, but it was not something he should surrender.

He said he hadn't looked at it that way and that he'd ride it out and ask John Ryan if they could have a meeting to chat about things. He rang three times to speak to Ryan and left messages that he'd like to make an appointment to speak to him.

Ryan rang back but said he was busy. The one afternoon they were both available, he had a prior appointment with a journalist. They never had the meeting and have never spoken since.

▽ J.D.

I always thought that if and when I turned to rugby league it would be as a result of a calm and carefully balanced decision. I had rejected Leeds in 1986 and St Helens in the summer of 1988 after considerable thought and although I had spoken often, and too loudly, about the temptations of going north it was not a move I intended to take lightly.

Yet in the end I decided to take the plunge almost in a split second. And it wasn't the money that pushed me over the edge. The money had been on offer from two or three clubs for the past few years and had been just a 'phone call away, and would probably be still waiting for another year or two.

What made up my mind for me was the sudden realisation that if I stayed I would be putting my rugby future in the hands of men I could no longer trust or respect.

Doug Laughton had been the first league coach who had actually come down to Wales to put his case face to face, and he didn't concentrate on the money or the security angle. He just told me that being a professional meant that I would get respect as well as reward. He explained the benefits of being with players and coaches who were all on the same wavelength and motivated by the same ambitions. It was a hard game but you got what your talent and effort deserved and no bungling amateur could take it away on some whim.

At that time, when my career and those of other players seemed to be at the mercy of the aimlessness affecting the administration of Welsh rugby, they were very persuasive words. But even then just one word of encouragement or support from Welsh selectors or coaches could have countered Doug's argument and convinced me that the task of putting Wales back on the winning trail was a challenge worth staying for. But I couldn't get them to look me in the eyes, let alone talk to me.

After a few days the buck was being passed to me by experts – I wish I could get the ball as quick. The press were quick to take up the theme but I wasn't worried about that so much as reading that John Dawes was fitting me up with the blame as well. Since he was the WRU's Director of Coaching and the convenor of the selection committee I thought he might have elected to share the flak with me, some of which was quite funny. One paper which had called me 'Captain Courageous' in New Zealand now called me 'Cap'n Calamity'.

What I wanted more than anything was a chat with John Ryan the Welsh coach. I'd always enjoyed a close relationship with coaches – Brian Thomas and Ron Waldron at Neath and Gareth Jenkins at Llanelli – and there's no problem in rugby that can't be solved by deciding on a common objective and working hard together to achieve it. And if it involved me losing the captaincy, I was prepared for it. But my calls went unanswered.

I even wrote out a letter containing my idea of the strongest Welsh team we could put out at that moment. It might have been a bit cheeky but I thought that every opinion would help. In the end I decided not to post it.

The next squad session was on the first Tuesday in January, the weekend after which the Welsh squad were going to Spain for a few days' get-together, and I thought we were bound to have a discussion about the Romanian game and all the press talk about the captaincy.

I had received a call from Doug Laughton over Christmas asking me if I was interested in joining Widnes. I wasn't very enthusiastic but he said he'd ring again. He had me watched in our game against Swansea on the Monday after New Year's Day and word had got out of Widnes's interest. I told the press that I was staying and all

I wanted was to restore the battered image of Welsh rugby 'whether as captain or not'.

We beat Swansea 38–15 and I played well enough as did Jonathan Griffiths who looked certain to play for Wales against Scotland because Robert Jones was getting over pneumonia.

It was said at the time that I went north to avoid the disgrace of having the captaincy taken off me following the Romanian defeat. But quite honestly I would have been relieved if they'd taken it from me. I just didn't see why I should give it up. I regarded the position as a great honour and I didn't see I had done anything that demanded I should relinquish it.

I knew I hadn't played well against Romania and that I made tactical errors but I would have made them whether or not I was captain. I choose the options I consider right, whoever is captain. When I was playing for Neath, where I was captain, or Llanelli, where I wasn't, I played the way that best suited the team, the conditions and the strength of the opposition.

But with Wales it is different, especially when you haven't a settled team. We hadn't been as convincing as we should have been against Western Samoa but, then again, they were very awkward customers and we couldn't get any pattern going. But nobody thought of discussing what went wrong, they just made a pile of changes including throwing Paul Thorburn out and bringing Tony Clement back. Then they dropped Mark Ring for being late, a decision that probably had more to do with our defeat than any other single reason, and instead of bringing in the experience of Bleddyn Bowen they brought in Mike Hall who hadn't played before.

The inconsistency and callousness of the selectors at this time reached a new low. After telling Mike Hall he couldn't play both for Cambridge in the Varsity match on the Tuesday and then for Wales on the Saturday they changed their minds and brought him in for cover when I was doubtful. Mike played in the Varsity match, as anyone would have, and naturally thought he would be overlooked for the Welsh match but, when Mark was disciplined for being late for training, Mike was brought straight into the team at the expense of Bleddyn who was in the squad as cover.

It was baffling and brutal all at once as Bleddyn was absolutely shattered by his treatment. Months later he asked a selector how such a thing could happen and was told, 'Ah, but you were only a convenience at the time.'

The public are not aware of such happenings and that there's so much farce going on behind the scenes. The players get the stick but they don't get much carrot.

The selectors who made all these decisions did not say a word to me about what our tactical approach should be against Romania. They must have had certain reasons for making the changes they did, they must have thought this player would be better for the team than that player, that a new pattern was needed. But they didn't explain to me what they were hoping to achieve.

After the match everybody knew exactly what tactics we should have employed. It is a shame they hadn't given me the benefit of their vast knowledge beforehand.

Great captains, I am told, should have the tactical know-how to vary the approach when they see things are going wrong. I agree. I made the mistake of thinking that since we were playing Romania, a team not yet in the forefront of world rugby, I would play similar tactics to those which had made us the top team in Britain earlier that year.

We would spread the ball wide and we would run and set up rucks and make the most of second phase possession. Not exactly original but something that a Welsh team playing at home should be able to handle. But although we ran the ball and set up the rucks, our forwards never arrived until after the Romanians did.

Had I scored an early penalty instead of hitting the post, had we scored from a break I made, had a forward not trodden on someone after we'd been awarded a penalty in front of the posts, we would have had a nice early lead and perhaps things would have been different. But we didn't and Romania got stronger in spirit and confidence and their outside half was getting some colossal touch kicks that bounced a yard inside. It was like being in the middle of a nightmare.

What I should have done, of course, was to change the pattern by kicking more, trying to keep them in their half. But for a Welsh team to be reduced to kicking its way out of trouble against an emerging team like Romania would have been a failure in itself. Under those circumstances a bad win is no more encouraging than a defeat.

I still think we played better than we had against Western Samoa. I felt we set up chances but didn't accept them. There was a lack of confidence in the side which I found worrying if understandable because of the backroom chaos.

As for the Romanians, they played to their strengths admirably.

They had a big pack and a fly-half who kicked brilliantly. They tackled well and got away with repeatedly taking our support players out. They didn't pass the ball once but I don't blame them for that. They were a lot stronger than we expected and while nothing we tried to do came off, they stuck to their guns and came away with a victory they will be celebrating for years.

We had advanced no further since New Zealand, in fact we'd gone backwards and it was a situation that reflected badly on everyone, not only me and the players but the selectors and coaches as well.

When I reached the Arms Park for the squad training on Tuesday night I was bursting to talk with John or the selectors. All I received from any of them was a formal nod or a quiet 'hello'. Nothing else was said and the atmosphere was screaming for somebody to say something. We just trained and left.

The only man in any sort of authority to have spoken to me since the Romania defeat had been John Dawes who asked me if I had thought of giving up the captaincy. I said I hadn't. I wonder now if he was just sounding me out on behalf of the selectors or whether it was just a personal question.

On the way home I started to think about what their intentions were. Perhaps they weren't going to say anything and just announce the team with someone else as captain. Perhaps if I didn't resign, they were going to leave me in the job. Perhaps they weren't even going to pick me at all.

I sat in the chair at home thinking how Thorburn and Bowen had been treated so deplorably and how Paul Moriarty had been ignored. How they hadn't even 'phoned Robert Jones when he was ill with pneumonia. Then I thought back to my debut for Wales, how it came about when Gareth Davies, after 21 caps, had been insulted when the name A N Other had appeared where his name had been.

It was near midnight when Doug Laughton rang. He said he had an offer I couldn't refuse. I said I didn't feel like talking about it. He said he wanted to come and see me next day. I said he'd be having a wasted journey.

'Fair enough,' he replied. 'But I want to be looking into your face when you tell me "No".'

150

14

Welcome to Widnes

There are times when it is difficult to suppress the mischievous thought that Widnes was originally called Wilderness but some of the letters corroded and dropped off.

Your impression of the place much depends on which way you approach it, and which way the wind is blowing. If you come from the south, from Runcorn, you pass the jumbled pipes and drums of acres of chemical works and cross the Mersey over a high-arched suspension bridge which looks as if it was assembled from a giant Meccano set.

The flat landscape is interrupted to the right by the eight cooling towers of the Fiddler's Ferry power station and straight ahead by a single smoke stack 400 feet high which, together with the West Bank Industrial Estate, does not make a pretty gateway to the town. And once in it you can search all day without finding a recognisable centre, apart from a haphazard sprawl of small shops.

There is a smell, too, which intermittently troubles the nostrils. This apparently comes from a knackers yard and is so readily absorbed into the everyday life of Widnes, only strangers seem to consider it worth mentioning.

None of this description, of course, tells you what the place is really like, or what a good job its 64,000 townspeople make of creating a strong and friendly identity from such unfavourable surroundings.

The rugby league club – appropriately called 'The Chemics' – is very much at the core of that identity and, certainly in the 'seventies and 'eighties, has contributed substantially to the town's pride. And it is a pride that comes not just by association but by direct and personal involvement.

Around 15 per cent of the Widnes population regularly turn up to watch the team play at Naughton Park, the present capacity of which is 16,000 and no longer adequate to cater for all who want to attend the big matches there. Even those who don't go, however, take an active interest in their fortunes by supporting the weekly prize draws which have been the basis of the club's finances.

Since the start of 1988 those weekly draws have been revitalised and now are raising money for the club at the rate of £200,000 a year. So successful are they that there's a waiting list for the chance to help the club and win one of the many and valuable weekly prizes. That, plus an upsurge from around 4000 average attendance in 1987 to 8648 in 1989 means that the townspeople literally have a stake in the success of the team.

And if they don't like the way the club is being run, they can take steps that would make most football club owners, whether soccer or rugby, go pale. Widnes RLFC is not owned by the archetypal rich benefactor, but is run by a committee of nine – all local people, some of them ex-players – who each serves three years. Every year, therefore, three of them retire or offer themselves for re-election by the club's season ticket holders, which in 1989 numbered 1888. Committee members seeking another term of office find it helpful to have at least one trophy on display when they offer themselves for reselection on ballot night.

The committee are a cross-section from local life and its members in the 1988/89 season were Mrs Audrey Spencer, who earns her place through her enthusiastic work as secretary of the Supporters' Club, Tom Smith, a former player and chairman, David Morgan, a South Walian who claims to have stopped off in Widnes to post a letter and has stayed ever since, Joe Preston, a buoyant blacksmith, Frank Nyland, a local solicitor who is the club's legal adviser, Jim Mills, former Widnes and Great Britain forward, Sammy Evans, a businessman with interests as varied as scrap-metal and nightclubs and Wilf Hunt, another former player and managing director of an engineering firm.

A chat with any of them, the president Colin Hirons or the chairman Ray Owen would reveal none of the pretensions that often walk hand in hand with official status in a successful club. 'It may sound corny,' says chairman Owen, a former scrum half with Wakefield and Widnes and now a publican, 'but we really are a club of the people. We were in danger of going under three years ago. It is their money that saved the club, and if they don't like the way we run it they soon tell us.'

When Jonathan joined them it was not a time when many complaints rang around the homely terraces of Naughton Park.

The club was founded in 1873 and was one of the original Northern rugby clubs who split from the Rugby Union in 1895 over the right to compensate their players for lost wages, thereby creating the Rugby League. However, it was not until the 1970s that Widnes became consistently a major force in the game. They may have taken their time to get to that point but once there they revelled in the honours. Between 1974 and 1984 they appeared seven times at Wembley in the Challenge Cup Final, a period also liberally sprinkled with success in the Championship, the John Player Trophy and the Premiership.

Some of the men who played a part on the field in that winning decade played as vital a role behind the scenes in the club's resurgence in the late 'eighties. Coach Doug Laughton was captain of Widnes and Great Britain in the 'seventies and became player-coach, only to resign in 1983 in order to sample what life was like without rugby league. In 1986 he was back as coach to find the club not in the best of financial states. Doug, like everyone else at Widnes, is a part-timer – he runs a successful heating business – and found himself using his own money to buy fish and chips for the team on the way home from an away match. And, on attendances of 3000, rebuilding the team was not something the club could reach into the pocket to do.

But Widnes were being directed towards a better future by men who armed Doug with the financial ammunition to put the finishing flourishes to his careful team construction. Reg Bowden, who had been with Widnes as a charismatic scrum half in the 'seventies, took over the club's fund raising and with another newcomer, secretary John Stringer, began to give the club a bustling and productive backroom.

Laughton has made a reputation for his ability to spot rugby union players with the mental and physical flexibility to switch codes successfully. But it is often overlooked that before the arrival of his spectacular converts he was choosing players wisely from the less likely reaches of the league. Hooker Phil McKenzie came from Second Division Rochdale and at the end of the 1988/89 season was named second best in the world in his position.

Joe Grima, a quick and powerful forward, was transferred in from Swinton and transformed as the Widnes team began to take shape around the nucleus of local talent the club has always been fortunate to find. Then Doug Laughton began to add the extra ingredients from union, starting with one of the most spectacular signings ever to change codes – winger Martin Offiah.

Doug had travelled to the Middlesex Sevens to watch another player but Offiah, then playing for Rosslyn Park, made an immediate impression because of his speed. Doug got a friend to telephone Rosslyn Park posing as a journalist to get Offiah's 'phone number. The player was persuaded to join Widnes for a bargain £40,000 and broke record after record as he established himself as perhaps the fastest ball carrier in the world.

Alan Tait was centre for Kelso and Scotland when he experienced the Laughton persuasion. But Alan needed no convincing of the values of league football because his father had played for Workington.

He, too, was a rapid success. Introduced to the game slowly but soon to shine, Alan was converted into a full back with stunning results. He had played barely 20 league matches when he joined Martin Offiah in the Great Britain team – and was named Man of the Match in an international against France.

Laughton's third signing was a result of long-distance judgement that was remarkable. He saw Emosi Koloto playing for Wellington in New Zealand against a Wales touring team on television. Doug was in a rain-battered holiday caravan in Anglesey at the time and the commentary was all in Welsh but he saw enough about the Tongan's play at No. 8 to decide upon an approach there and then.

To sell a future in rugby league with Widnes over the telephone to a Tongan in New Zealand is an achievement fit for the record books. Although transfer of ability from code to code is much more difficult for a forward, Koloto finished the 1988/89 season as yet another one of Laughton's successes.

Jonathan was to be Laughton's fourth plunge into the union ranks and his biggest risk, because Jonathan was far more firmly established as a world star than the others and therefore would command a much bigger signing on fee. And the bigger the outlay, the more face to lose from a mistake.

But Doug had had his eye on him long before he had seen any of his other signings. When Jonathan made his debut for Wales against England in April 1985 he was watching the match on television in a pub. Doug wasn't directly involved in the game at the time but Jonathan caught his eye immediately. 'That boy can play,' he said, to no-one in particular.

By the time Laughton came back into rugby with Widnes he had seen further glimpses of the Davies class on television but knew that there was no way Widnes could afford him. So convinced was he that Jonathan would make a great rugby league player he recommended him to Wigan.

'I told their chairman that he was the best thing around and since they could afford him, they should buy him. They may have been rivals but we couldn't afford him and I just wanted to see him in our game. I knew it would be good for the league and good for him,' recalls Laughton.

But Jonathan resisted all offers to turn, so Doug just kept an eye on him, dispatching his chief scout Eddie McDonnell to watch him in club rugby while he maintained televised supervision of Jonathan's Welsh appearances.

If Doug needed any confirmation of the player's suitability for league it came in that second Test match out in New Zealand. 'He was tackling two men at a time,' said Doug, 'and those All Blacks are not that easy to stop. He was the only Welshman to come out of that tour with honour.'

Doug noted that Jonathan rejected St Helen's offer when he returned from New Zealand and calculated that he would probably want to stay in union at least until after the British Lions tour of Australia in the summer of 1989. So he put his interest on ice.

Then came the Romanian match and Doug couldn't believe the criticism Jonathan was taking. So around Christmas he gave him a reconnoitring telephone call. The response was not exactly encouraging but Doug sensed it was worth persevering. He asked the committee to consider making an offer.

It probably seemed an odd request. The team had won the Championship and the Premiership the previous season and at that time were already in the John Player Trophy final and well in line for every other honour. The urgency to spend a record fee to strengthen the squad was not apparent. Doug argued that a player of Jonathan's calibre did not become available often. Indeed, he might not be available at all. But if he was, then they should invest some of the money the club was making.

'I don't have the slightest doubt he will make it and if he is going to come up here then we ought to have him in our squad. Just think of the cash as a short-term loan. I guarantee we'll soon get back every penny through the turnstiles,' Doug told the committee, who were swayed into supporting their coach's quest.

Doug spoke to Jonathan again after he had played for Llanelli against Swansea on Monday 2 January. The Widnes man talked loosely about finance but concentrated on offering a better appreciation of his talents than he was receiving from his countrymen at that time, stressing that he would find league a better and more consistent vehicle for his skills.

'People say I can sell fridges to the Eskimos, which is nonsense,' says Laughton, 'but I could sell them fan heaters, because they want them. I was selling something I firmly believed in and what Jonathan needed. I was trying to offer something his game wasn't giving him.'

There were two other factors on Laughton's side. If Jonathan was going to be of full value to any league club that season, he would have to sign by that weekend, i.e. 9 January in order to qualify for the Challenge Cup competition. So any team with aspirations of Wembley would hesitate to pay big money after that for a player who would be unavailable to help them win the most glittering prize in the game. (Doug later confessed he would have snapped up Jonathan regardless of his eligibility for the Cup, but he neglected to tell the committee or Jonathan.)

The other pressure was applied by Wales, who were due to leave for a coaching get-together in Spain on Friday 6 January. If Jonathan was going north, he was honour-bound to withdraw from the squad in time for them to select a replacement.

So a quick decision was necessary and even though he put forward an attractive offer and had made some convincing points about Jonathan's present position and the great prospects awaiting him, Doug felt he was fighting a losing battle.

'Despite all his talk about turning to league one day, deep down he didn't want to leave home. And for all his supposed arrogance he wasn't sure he would succeed if he came. My hardest job was to convince him he could make it. "Are you sure?" he kept asking. The funny thing was I didn't really need him. I wasn't a desperate coach trying to sign someone who could revitalise my struggling team. I had the best team already. I just knew that it was in both our long-term interests if he joined us there and then,' remembers Doug.

When Jonathan returned late on Tuesday night from the ill-fated Welsh squad session Doug telephoned him to say he wanted to travel down and 'make him an offer he couldn't refuse'. Jonathan sounded a bit downcast and replied, 'You'll be wasting your time coming.' Doug said he wanted to be looking in his eyes when Jonathan turned him down and added, 'If you do, I promise you won't ever see or hear from me again. Just give me an hour of your time and that'll be it, one way or another.'

Jim Mills, the Widnes committee man and former playing colleague of Doug in both the Widnes and Great Britain teams, was asked to accompany Doug. Jim was born in Cardiff and went north when still a teenager. He was well-known in Wales, not only as a good player but a fearsome one with a record of over 20 sending-offs to his name – what goes on among rugby league forwards in the privacy of their own battles not always being appreciated by referees. But a more affable and charming giant you couldn't wish to meet.

This was not the first signing foray Jim had accompanied Doug on. In the early 'eighties they had gone to Neath to watch winger Elgan Rees and were in the clubhouse after the match when Doug was asked to leave. 'And take that big thug with you,' said the Neath man pointing at Jim. 'I will, as long as you tell him,' replied Doug.

Rugby league men are used to the understandable ire of union people, but Doug and Jim came close to another embarrassing confrontation when they travelled down to see Jonathan on the Wednesday.

They had spent a few hours with him and had left him to muse over their discussions while they travelled to Barry where they were to spend the night with Jim's father. All the talking had made them thirsty so they stopped at the first pub they came to in Llanelli. Jim immediately recognised the man who came to serve them as they reached the bar. It was Norman Gale, the former Llanelli hooker, whose pub they had unwittingly chosen. Norman knew Jim and once they had exchanged greetings, Jim introduced Doug.

Norman looked at them suspiciously. 'What are you doing down here?' he asked pointedly. Jim thought quickly, 'We're down to have a word with Tony Clement,' he lied, not really explaining why they had to come to Llanelli in order to see a Swansea player.

While they chatted Jim was trying frantically to remember if Norman was still connected with Llanelli. In the end he asked him. 'Yes,' said Norman, 'I'm the chairman.'

Doug quietly choked on his beer. Of all the men to meet, the chairman of the club from whom they were trying to steal the star player was not the most appropriate.

Not that they were all that confident. Jim recalls that Doug put their chances no higher than 50–50 on the journey down and even after hours of discussion a deal was far from certain.

Doug had tried to bring the negotiations to an end by asking Jonathan to name a price he would have to consider. Jonathan, after much delay, finally named a figure he thought might drive Widnes away.

'You'd come for that?' Doug asked deliberately.

'I'm 99 per cent certain I would,' Jonathan replied.

Later, Doug rang his chairman Ray Owen. 'You'd better have a committee meeting,' he said, naming the figure Jonathan had mentioned. 'We don't need a meeting because the committee will support your decision either way,' said Ray.

Doug ruminated with Jim on the whole business. That was the first time he'd seen Jonathan in the flesh. He had seen him play only on television. But the object of his long talks was to find out as much about the player as Jonathan was finding out about league and Widnes. 'Had he been a toffee-nosed little git or if he hadn't displayed the right sort of character and honesty I would have pulled out of it there and then. But everything was right,' said Doug.

At half past midnight on Thursday 5 January he rang Jonathan. 'You're on,' he said.

▽ J.D.

It was like being dead and reading your own obituaries in the newspapers. People were talking gravely about how much I would be missed and what a tragedy it was. Llanelli players said how they were training with me the previous night and never suspected I would go just like that.

I suppose I was dead in a way. As far as Welsh rugby was concerned I had ceased to exist. I was a non-person, to be talked about in the past tense.

Considering the sort of press I had been receiving since the Romanian game the transformation was amazing. People say lovely things when you're gone; it's a shame that they don't say them when you're still around.

I was grateful for the way Gerald Davies summed it all up in *The Times* when he traced the reasons for my disillusion and ended, 'those who have attempted to deny him his rightful place will now ponder long and hard at the gap his departure leaves'.

Stephen Jones in the *Sunday Times* was another who was generous, writing: 'He has never been embraced as warmly by Wales as have the others in the great rolling dynasty of fly-halves, especially the legendary, almost mystical, Barry John. Yet for me Davies was unquestionably the greatest of all, the richest and the complete talent. His single greatest failing is that he was born at the wrong time.'

But Barry John himself wrote in the *Daily Express*, 'No-one doubts Davies's great skills and spontaneous attitude on the field. But I believe the Welsh public will remember him only for his potential and what could have been had he stayed.'

But who knows what would have happened had I stayed. I might have been flung out like so many others. I might have become just another victim of the people who controlled my international career.

There was much speculation about the reason that finally sent me north. I have tried to give the real reason in the previous chapter but the theory that persisted longest was that I was afraid I would lose the captaincy. But I don't even know now whether I would have lost it.

But one thing I am sure about – I deliberately misled nobody by continually denying that I was on the point of turning. I denied that Widnes had approached me because I didn't want any speculation about a course of action I had no intention of taking. And I can assure anyone who felt upset at the lack of warning that the four people most surprised by my decision were my wife Karen, my mother, my mother-in-law and me.

Karen had decided to go back to work at the hospital once Scott was old enough to be left with her mother. She actually started on the Tuesday morning without the slightest idea that 48 hours later her comeback would be over. My mother was convinced I wasn't going and, because I hadn't been able to get through after my sudden change of mind, she was cheerfully telling reporters not to be silly when they were ringing up for reaction from her. Karen's mother Virene was similarly stunned. I had trained with the Llanelli boys on Wednesday little thinking I would no longer be one of them within a few hours.

This book was already being put together and I had spent an hour earlier that day outlining to Peter the reasons why I was turning down another league offer so that he could scribble out my thoughts while they were fresh in my mind. I rang him first thing next morning to warn him that I would be changing those thoughts for a new set.

That's how it happened. So swiftly, the decision was in my mind even before I knew it was there. I apologise to anyone who considers I misled them. I still believe that if anyone from the WRU had spoken to me on that Tuesday night and discussed the situation and how we could best seek an improvement, or even if someone had put a sympathetic hand on my shoulder and said something encouraging, I would have found it very difficult to accept Widnes's offer. But the only friendly, convincing and supportive words I heard that week were from Doug Laughton and Jim Mills. They were the professionals and suddenly I felt it necessary to join them.

I hadn't expected the event to pass unnoticed but experienced observers at both ends of the transaction said they had seen nothing like the media excitement. In Wales, of course, all the radio and television channels are duplicated to cater for the Welsh and English audiences. So we faced double the number of local interviews even before the national cameras and microphones began to crowd into Virene's front room in Cefneithin and through Mammy's door in Trimsaran.

The newspapers, of course, were something else. The size of my fee got bigger by £1000 a minute and there was headline after headline and page after page debating why I had gone and whether I had done the right thing. I tried to read as much of it as I could but I had to give up in the end. My favourite cutting from those few days was a letter to *The Times* from a gentleman in Berkshire which read:

'Sir, couldn't Wales keep Jonathan Davies and sell the selectors to Widnes?'

There were a couple of incidents that seem funny now but were not so at the time. The *Sun* newspaper contacted me just after I signed, offering me £5000 if I would 'slag off' the Welsh Rugby Union. I turned them down and paid the penalty, because they immediately signed up the ready mouth of former Welsh and Pontypool hooker Bobby Windsor to write an article headed 'Good Riddance to Selfish Davies'. It appeared the *Sun* didn't mind who was slagging whom off, as long as someone did and Bobby must have needed the money.

One of the many pressmen who came to interview me was John Taylor, the former London Welsh and Wales flanker who writes for the *Mail on Sunday*. John wanted to spend the next few days by my side and write about my experiences in Sunday's edition. But I said I felt so hemmed in I wasn't happy to do that.

He then wrote a piece saying I was a 'bit of a grizzler'.

I suppose people have to have fixed images about places, but my first impressions of Widnes were very favourable. Admittedly it was dark when we drove up from South Wales on the Friday evening. I was only going up for a couple of nights to be introduced and watch Widnes play in the John Player Special Trophy against Wigan at Bolton, so it seemed hardly worth dragging Karen and Scott up. We would move up as a family the following week.

After all the media attention in the 24 hours since I finally signed on the Thursday, it was a relief to be getting away from it. Ken had agreed to come up with me and Peter, and they were chatting away in the front as I sat in the back reflecting on what still seemed a dream. I have to confess that the misgivings which were later to reach panic level began to take shape in the car as we headed north and despite my frequent reassurances to my companions that I was feeling good and really looking forward to getting there, I just didn't know what to expect.

But the northern suburbs of Widnes as we turned off the M62 looked just like any other town and as we turned into the car park of the Hillcrest Hotel, which was to be my home for the next month or so, we were pleasantly surprised. No sooner had I taken my first step out of the car when my hand was being shaken by a couple of passing lads, and the welcome was just as warm inside as we walked in to surroundings less austere than we had anticipated and certainly nothing like the Widnes image.

We walked into the restaurant bar to be greeted by palm trees and smart cane furniture and a large brass-topped bar into which a piano had been built. The pianist was tinkling gently away as we sipped our pints from tall thin glasses that would have been denounced as poncy back in Trimsaran.

It was like being in Hollywood and, since all of Widnes's recruits stay there courtesy of the owner Harold Nelson, the place has done wonders in making the newcomers feel at home. The food is excellent and the staff so friendly we felt quite sad when we eventually moved into our new home a few miles away. It was just as well we went, though, because Scott had been spoiled rotten, and so had Karen and I.

That evening, the first person I saw was Emosi Koloto, the Tongan who had once flattened my brother-in-law and whom I had last played against for Wales against Wellington in New Zealand. While Emosi was telling me how he was settling down, in came Eddie McDonnell, the chief scout who had stood incognito on so many terraces in South Wales watching me over the previous year or so.

Then Doug came in, and Jim Mills, the chairman Ray Owen, secretary John Stringer and solicitor Frank Nyland. I hadn't met any of the club officials before and in no time it had developed into a lively welcome party. The only problem was that the telephone never stopped ringing with calls from media and well-wishers. Since the noise in the bar had become a touch deafening I kept having to go out into the foyer to take the calls.

On one of these visits I bumped into a boy I recognised as centre with one of the major Welsh clubs. He wasn't a big name but he was a good player. He looked as if he'd been in a fight. His nose seemed to have been ripped off and stuck back on again. It turned out he'd come up to have a secret trial with Hull and they had put him in the 'A' team at Swinton that night. He'd found it hard going.

I asked him if he was going to move up but he felt the terms weren't good enough to tempt him. It was pure coincidence that he'd been booked into that hotel before returning home the next day. I felt a bit embarrassed as he trooped off to bed. Here was I being feted like a hero and here was he having a lonely night after a miserable experience at playing rugby for a living.

Almost as an indication that I had nothing to feel secure about, Doug made a great show of presenting me with a Widnes shirt in the bar. It had No. 14 on the back – a subtle hint that a substitute's jersey was all I was entitled to at that time. It was three o'clock before I got to bed and I was in no state for the black pudding that Ken was enjoying in the morning.

I was anxious to meet the rest of my new team-mates but Doug was purposely keeping me away from the team. Saturday was, after all, a big day for them. They had fought their way to the final of the John Player and didn't deserve to have their thunder stolen. But not even Doug had anticipated the strength of the ballyhoo my signing was causing.

I had to attend a press conference organised by the Rugby League before the final and I was to get there at midday. John Stringer picked us up with plenty of time for the 30-minute journey up the motorway and all the way we were continually being beeped at and every car that passed us seemed to be full of people waving at me. I didn't think I was that well known. It was only when I got out of the car at Bolton that I realised it had Widnes RLFC emblazoned all over it.

A traffic hold-up delayed our arrival at Burnden Park and we had barely come to a halt in the car park when the door was opened and I was yanked out to start posing for about 50 photographers. David Howes, the League's very efficient public relations officer, then rescued me, explaining that the press conference was getting restless. I was pushed through a great scrum of people and led into a room that must have had about 60 reporters crammed wall to wall. David took me to a raised dais at the end of the room, where there was a microphone, and announced, 'Gentlemen, Jonathan Davies, rugby league's biggest ever signing.' There was even a smattering of applause. Then David stepped away and I suddenly felt very alone.

I'd given press conferences before, but they were after matches when I was one of a few people being questioned and I knew what I was talking about. But now I was staring at the hard-bitten faces of every rugby league writer in the land and a good few up from London as well. I don't quite know how I got through it but I managed to conceal my hopeless ignorance about rugby league which, as I told them, I had seen in the flesh only once before.

I refused to discuss the fee, and I said I had no idea where Doug Laughton was going to play me and didn't mind as long as it wasn't in the forwards. I told them I got my speed from fear and I should have added that judging how frightened I was, I was going to be a lot faster in league than I was in union.

After that it was out on the pitch to be interviewed live on *Grandstand* and then face a dozen other television and radio interviews. Even though it was drizzling with rain, the photographers insisted on my putting on a Widnes shirt and posing for them again.

Then I was whipped away to attend a lunch given by Widnes's sponsors ICI, only we got there too late for lunch and after meeting a lot of people it was back to the stadium where I was introduced to the crowd amid a lot of cheering and chanting. If I had been a Widnes player listening to that lot from the dressing room I would have been pissed off. I was getting all the attention, they were going to have to do all the work.

I sat in the stand next to John Stringer who was going to explain a few of the finer points to me. I was asked later if John had been helpful to me. I replied that I couldn't hear much because he had his head in hands most of the time.

It was not one of Widnes's better days. I now realise why they were so disappointed. I haven't seen them play that badly. Wet conditions were to prove the team's undoing in one or two later games and on that day their handling went to pieces. Wigan beat them 12–6 and that looks a lot closer than it was. I don't believe the Widnes boys were bothered by all the attention lavished on me but Wigan certainly claimed later that it made them all the more determined to remind people how well they could play the game. No-one did that better than Ellery Hanley. It was my first sight of him and I was very impressed.

After the match, in a crowded lounge that seemed to contain every rugby league coach there was, I finally met the Widnes team. It was hardly a joyous occasion but they were very genuine in their welcomes and good wishes.

I must say that nearly everybody in the place came up to wish me well and to say how pleased they were that I had come up north. It struck me that evening that it wasn't just Widnes who were pleased to see me, every club in the League was glad I was there. There were times in the next three months when they found funny ways of showing it, but I hadn't realised how much rugby league feels isolated.

I suppose it comes from years of being regarded by the rest of the country as some sort of inferior version of rugby, and looked down upon by the Rugby Union as being tarnished by money. So whenever a top player from union joins their ranks it is like a victory for them. Since I cost more than anyone else I seemed to represent a major victory. The game had been making big strides for a few years and my arrival was proof that they had an attraction that was getting through to all parts of the game and the country.

It didn't do much to relieve the burden I felt on my shoulders but I was very touched. I had thought of my signing only as it affected me and the Widnes club, but I had soon realised that every transfer from union to league was a bonus for them as a whole. I certainly felt I wasn't going to remain an alien for long – as long as I could produce the goods, that is.

Another myth was about to be wrecked that night. In union the word is that rugby league doesn't have a social side – it is just not true and I began to find that out pretty quickly.

We all climbed aboard the coach outside the Bolton ground, players and committee, and stopped at the pub in Warrington they always stop at on the way home from an away game. Then we called in at the social club at the ground so that the supporters could have a drink with us. Then we went to Jim Mills' night club where a buffet and dance was laid on.

There was a certain lack of the party spirit but Doug got on the mike and made a little speech saying that they might well have played like a load of nellies but let's have a good time now and we'll talk about it later.

The fuss and ballyhoo over my signing didn't die down for a few weeks after that. Nerves and tension over the next seven days before my debut were to cost me 12lbs in weight. But at the moment, at least, I felt I'd seen an attitude to rugby that wasn't unfamiliar.

15
Free to Earn

Jonathan had to face much more than a massed media onslaught in his first frantic weeks as a rugby league man. He had to contend with a more valuable facet of his sudden launch into the nation's attention – the freedom to earn an honest pound from his fame.

Let us not pretend that he hadn't picked up a penny or two, from what are politely called peripheral earnings, while he was in union, but it was nothing substantial. From an early age in a player's life that code preaches a solid line in warning its players to treat the proffered pound as Eve should have treated the serpent's apple.

But all restrictions, moral or otherwise, were swept away by his move to Widnes and opportunities soon abounded to collect more off the field of play than he would earn on it.

An agent appeared at his side as if through a trap-door. Exciting pictures were painted of profit potential, starting with an offer to model the latest in men's fashions for a major tailoring firm.

Wisely, Jonathan heeded those around him who counselled that the first sight the public should have of him in his new role ought to be in the fetching white and black shouldered ensemble of Widnes RLFC, rather than in something more trendy but less expressive of his suitability for the rigours of his new profession.

It says a lot for him that he was able to keep his head as these financial temptations competed for his attention like sideshow barkers. There were times when he eyed the flood of money on offer like a kid let loose in a sweet shop, which is not surprising considering the lack of cash-shaped confectionery in his life hitherto, but decorum and restraint scored notable victories over greed as he tried desperately to concentrate on getting stuck into his new game.

It helped to have his family on hand. A sense of perspective is more easily maintained when mealtimes are shared with your wife and mother-in-law and when your six-month-old son is intent on uprooting every plant in the Hillcrest Hotel dining room.

His concern for his kinsfolk can be quite touching. When we arrived at Bolton and he was swept up in a great tide of photographers, well-wishers and autograph hunters and borne almost bodily towards his press conference, he turned and shouted over the heads, 'Peter, look after Ken.'

Ken, his stepfather, is a man in his mid-fifties not noticeably vulnerable. When he was 18 he was helping the Welsh Regiment look after a section of front line in the Korean war, so my protection seemed unnecessary. But it showed that even at that time of personal stress Jonathan had time to worry about someone else – someone, furthermore, who had been sent up ostensibly to look after him.

The pressure of that day and the succeeding week cannot be over-emphasised. Ray French, who played with distinction in both codes and who is now a leading writer and commentator on league, cannot recall such an explosion of interest. He and Jack MacNamara of the *Manchester Evening News*, doyen of the rugby league writing world, consider that it eclipsed the sensation over the signings of Welshmen Lewis Jones in 1952 and David Watkins in 1967, if only for the fact that media people are more numerous and vociferous these days.

Anyone not familiar with the ways of the media could easily be confused by the variety of demands and the inconsistency of payment. Most television and radio channels pay an interview fee but newspaper reporters and photographers pay only for exclusive material. When you are shivering in a rugby shirt, leaning out from the catwalk of a windswept Widnes bridge in order to satisfy the artistic demands of a cameraman, you may be entitled to enquire if you are getting paid for it or doing it for pleasure.

Hence there were one or two complaints that he was money-grabbing, an accusation that would not be supported by 99 per cent of the media men and women who helped to pester him out of nearly a stone in weight during his first ten days.

The cash he earned from the media interest was supplemented by offers from commercial concerns to open shops or appear at functions. His search for a house was complicated by a series of offers from builders anxious to include him as a dweller on one of the many new housing estates being built around north Cheshire at the time. Jonathan chose a Welsh-based firm who sold him a four-bedroom detached on the excellent Westbrook estate on the Widnes-Warrington borders. He was also inundated with offers of cars, rather ironically since he had another year of his driving ban to serve. He already had a car supplied by a Cardiff firm, with his and their names emblazoned on the side, but local garages wanted him to have one of theirs. After being driven around the local dealers by Jim Mills he eventually selected a Peugeot which Karen would use around Widnes, saving the Cardiff car for their visits back home to South Wales.

'Shall we arrange for a Birmingham garage to give you one as well, in case you want to pop in for a cup of tea on the way home?' asked Jim dryly as he recalled that he didn't even have a bike when he went north.

The trappings of Jonathan's new life were surrounding him with more rewards in a couple of months than he had previously gained in years – and that was before taking into account the earnings from his contract with Widnes.

Jonathan intends the details of that contract to remain a private matter between him and the club but emphasises that most of the estimates as to its worth are wildly over the top, largely because the press have tried to guess how much he would earn from all sources over the three and a half years of his contract. This includes bonuses for winning titles and cups, bonuses for being selected for Great Britain and peripheral earnings. A wild stab could hoist the figure up into the £300,000 range.

But the actual signing on fee is much less than that, certainly well under £200,000, even though it is a world record. And it represents a chance of security for the Davies family only if he can save that sum over the next few years and live off his week by week earnings. So many players have turned to rugby league for a large sum only to find that through failure to play well, or through injury or being in a losing team, their opportunities to earn a living wage from the game and its associated activities are limited and they have had to live off their signing on fees.

Say a player changes codes for a fee of £100,000 for a four-year contract. He will most probably receive a down payment of £20,000 and eight six-monthly instalments of £10,000, which are payable whether or not he makes the grade or receives a serious injury. The club will also help to find him a job which is not likely to be particularly lucrative unless he has qualifications.

Wages vary but at most First Division clubs for ordinary games are around £200 for a win, £40 for a defeat and an away draw brings the winning bonus, a home draw the losing money. Higher bonuses are on offer for big Cup ties or championship deciders.

These payments are paid to the first team plus the two substitutes. The 16th man receives a proportion of whatever the team earn, and injured players likewise. Therefore, there is not a lot available for a convert who doesn't make the grade, takes his time to adjust, gets hurt or belongs to a struggling team. Too many recent signings have come under one or another of these categories – Terry Holmes and David Bishop are two examples.

On the brighter side, recent advancement in the appeal and national awareness of league is bringing much better rewards for the top players. And improvement in British standards has led to a greater demand from Australia for players to go out there to play in our summer. Ellery Hanley and Martin Offiah are the two big names to be signed but several others have also been snapped up for fees ranging from £20,000 to £50,000 for a three-month spell.

At the end of his first season Jonathan had not established a fixed berth in the Widnes team but he had played in 12 full matches, plus four as substitute, and scored over 100 points. It was a good start but he realised more than anyone that whatever proportion he actually collects of the fortune that has been extravagantly forecasted for him, he'll earn every penny.

▽ J.D.

I was a professional rugby footballer long before I moved to rugby league. In fact, there are very few leading rugby union players entitled to be called amateurs.

I never earned money from actually playing rugby – but I earned it from being a player, and it seems to me that the Unions take a conveniently haphazard view of what constitutes an amateur. I don't mean the Unions of countries like New Zealand or France where they have long dropped any pretence that their top players don't get considerable rewards from the game. I mean the home countries, England and Wales in particular.

One day in 1988 I attended a rugby union match in England, not to play but to say a few words to a crowd of well-lubricated gentlemen. Afterwards I was given £400, which I did not mention to anyone apart from the Inland Revenue.

I've often thought that if the Inland Revenue were ever to make public the income tax returns of rugby union players, British Rail would have to lay on extra north-bound trains to cope with the rush. But the Revenue keeps faith with its customers and rugby union can carry on with the myth that it is an amateur game, keeping at bay the evils of commercialism.

In 1987, while I was in the process of moving from Neath to Llanelli I was approached by two well known England clubs, one in London and the other in the Midlands. It was the early days of the new leagues in England and they each offered me a good job, a house and a car if I would join them. Obviously, I rejected both of them but quite a few players have moved since the leagues came in and while I am not suggesting they all received the professional inducements I was offered, I am sure some of them did.

Some day, someone is going to have to explain to me what is the difference in principle between Widnes's offer and those I received from the two union clubs. In each case they were an attempt to persuade me to move by offering financial rewards, and they differ only in degree. I may say that, apart from the West Wales club I mentioned in an earlier chapter, I have never been offered an inducement to join a Welsh club.

Not that it offended me to receive that £400 or be offered jobs by English clubs. I don't think the game would suffer if these incidents could take place in the open. I received cash payments on other occasions, too, but the opportunities for being paid for making commercial appearances are limited in Wales because the risks of being reported are much too strong.

In London and the Midlands the opportunities are far more plentiful. Some players' names pop up on dinner menus more often than Norfolk turkey and I suspect, and hope, they get a good whack for being there.

It would not stretch the highly elastic definition of amateurism if players could be allowed to accept payment for activities around the game if not in it. Permission to accept peripheral earnings is by no means a new suggestion. It has been made and rejected several times in the past few years.

But the point the Unions conveniently ignore is that it is not a plea for something to be introduced, it is a plea for it to be condoned. The players want to be honest men. They want an accepted practice, which everybody knows is going on, to be brought into the open and have the guilt taken away.

In the spring of 1989 a survey was conducted which showed pretty clearly what the players feel about it all. The Coca Cola Sports magazine interviewed 40 top union players from England and Wales, including 30 internationals, on their attitudes to payments in the game. The vast majority (85 per cent to 15 per cent) said they would NOT like to see the game develop along fully professional lines although 60 per cent would accept a part-time commitment, being paid on a match-by-match basis.

But 100 per cent wanted a relaxation in the rules so that they could earn money from writing books, attending functions, sponsorships etc. And 100 per cent would welcome financial compensation for time off work while on international duty. A number lose money while representing their country. When I was on tour we received £15 a day expenses which didn't cover telephone calls home. This is obviously ridiculous. A lower number, 72 per cent, were happy that any money thus earned from the game should be put into a trust for when they retire.

I would have thought that such an overwhelming body of opinion from the elite of the game should have commanded some respect from the authorities. But they were dismissed out of hand by Dudley Wood, secretary of the RFU.

'Amateurism is about playing without any financial reward and we are determined the game will remain amateur,' he is quoted as saying. 'If a player loses money from work through playing the game, then that is unfortunately the sacrifice that has to be made.'

The sacrifices seem a little one-sided and as a rugby union player I used to find it difficult to accept being lectured on how important it was for me not to receive a penny to play the game by someone being paid a handsome wage to run it. I like Dudley Wood but he is in the odd position of being paid to preserve amateurism.

His counterpart on the Welsh RU used to be Ray Williams who made the same speeches about amateurism when he was in office. But Ray resigned after he, too, lost patience with the Union's outdated attitude to the facts of modern life. After he left he came out strongly in favour of players being allowed to cash in on the commercial side of the game.

Perhaps Dudley Wood ought to consider which is the most important part of his job, preserving amateurism or promoting rugby as an appealing game to play and watch.

New Zealand and France are two countries who have led the world recently in showing how well the game can be played. At the same time they have completely disregarded the same rules that Dudley Wood and his colleagues are determined to stick to.

If they don't want to follow the same road as the All Blacks perhaps our Unions should refuse to play them any more, thus saving the players the sort of humiliation the Welsh suffered there in 1988. While they're at it they may as well cut the French off the fixture list, too, because we've recently had the farcical situation of the French rugby league people complaining that French union were pinching all their best players by offering them more money.

Our Unions could just play each other and be happy in their mediocrity and go to bed every night feeling holy.

I was once invited on to a television programme to debate these very points with Peter Yarrington, a former RAF, Wasps and England wing forward who became a leading figure in the RFU. To say our views were different is putting it mildly – we were like people from different planets. He obviously wasn't going to take any nonsense from this little Welsh whippersnapper and I soon realised that it wasn't a game he was arguing about, it was a way of life.

Rugby union can be such a cosy and privileged existence if you come from the right background, or go to the right university and end up in one of the professions. The game is a great outlet and a great advantage in those circumstances. You tend to play for a fashionable club, meet all the right people and graduate to the committee. Cash rewards are fairly meaningless in that situation, but you have still benefited from the game. It doesn't really matter whether you get a bundle of tenners pressed into your hand or whether the game gives you a social status that helps you earn a living. Either way, you are cashing in on being a rugby player.

Last year Peter Yarrington became chairman of the Sports Council, a part-time position which carries an annual fee of £12,000 as compensation for taking him away from his normal occupation as head of a sports and leisure complex in London. It was the issue of paying players for taking time off work, the great 'broken time' row, that led to northern clubs breaking away from the Union and forming the Rugby League in 1895.

It is ironic that one of England's top union men is in line to accept what is virtually a 'broken time' payment.

I don't know if Mr Yarrington feels that all his success in life would still have come if he hadn't been a good rugby player. I am sure that my last two employers in South Wales, Neil O'Halloran and Gerallt Davies of Sterling, gave me a job because I was a well-known rugby player and for no other reason. I think I earned my pay but I doubt if I would have been valuable to them as mere Jonathan Davies, ex-painter and bulldozer basher of Trimsaran.

The only men in rugby who can fairly claim to be amateurs are those who work at something rugby didn't get for them – doctors and farmers come most easily to mind. Farmers make very suitable rugby men because they are strong and fit even before they start training. Walking around all day with a sheep under each arm gives them a great advantage over players with a soft job who have to beg or borrow time from their employers or family to maintain a high standard of fitness.

I have been asked if I would have turned to league if the rules involving peripheral earnings had been relaxed. At the time I received that illicit £400 I had been receiving plenty of invitations to earn money on the side. But because I felt they were watching me like hawks following my outburst about wanting to be paid, it was all too risky.

But there is no doubt there is a lot of money on offer and I don't doubt that many players are taking advantage. I should think a figure of between £10,000 and £15,000 a year could be comfortably earned by a rugby union player able to put himself about. A lot of people take advantage of union players because they are amateurs.

But if they legalised it, then writing books and newspaper columns, making public appearances, getting sponsorship from sportsgood firms could easily bring a top player over £30,000 a year. Obviously that would have made a big difference to my feelings about going north. I'm not saying I still wouldn't have been dissatisfied with the running of the game but with players able to earn a good living, attitudes to the game would be more professional, like they are in New Zealand.

Although I am not affected any more I would still like to see the change come for the sake of the game. But I can't see the powers in British rugby relenting, because it is not so much amateurism they are trying to preserve, they are preserving themselves.

16
Banned by Wales

At 8.35 p.m. on 20 January 1989, a rugby ball crashed through the kitchen window of Mrs Annie Goodwin, making history as well as a mess. The ball had started its journey flying through the posts at the 'cowshed' end of Naughton Park and bringing to Jonathan his first points in rugby league.

It was a reserve match against Hull five days after his brief debut against Salford, and Jonathan took the conversion kick bang in front of the posts where Andy Eyres had thoughtfully placed his try.

As he lined up, Jonathan heard one of the Hull players shout from behind the posts. 'At £250,000 he'd better not miss this boogar.'

The beef he thereupon applied to the ball was far and away too excessive and the ball climbed into the night sky and into the streets behind the ground before landing in Mrs Goodwin's kitchen. It is just as well she is the club's laundry lady and understood the importance in his getting off the mark. And since she got a double glazed window out of it, Jonathan's shirt is just as clean as the others.

The attendance for that reserve match was 4090 – not a massive crowd but a record nevertheless for an 'A' team game which normally attracted a couple of hundred. Such was the interest aroused by Jonathan's arrival the urge to see him in action was great.

But, even allowing for the conversion, the first half was not a convincing demonstration of skills worthy of a world record fee. He was playing at full back and found it difficult to get into the game. At half-time he was switched to stand-off and the transformation was spectacular and immediate. Within four minutes of the restart a sudden surge took him past three men and he sent in Paul Haughton for a try.

174

Eight minutes later he spun a beautiful reverse pass into the arms of Andy Eyres for another try and then slammed over the conversion from near the touchline. He rounded off his display by alerting David Myers to stand by for a low kick through and he put the ball perfectly 25 yards across the line for the young winger to pounce on.

Jonathan was made Man of the Match for his efforts, an honour that brought him £20 to go with his win bonus of £40, rugby not being a lucrative profession for reserves.

Later that night in the Hillcrest, Jonathan's pleasure at completing his first full league game so successfully was slightly marred by a friendly but forceful discussion on tackling.

In union, complaining to a brilliant outside half about his tackling is like moaning at Beethoven because he won't help to shift the piano and many have completed illustrious careers without bothering overmuch with the tiresome duty. But in league, tackling is so basic to the team's needs that everyone has to do his whack, and the more whacks the better.

But the complaint about Jonathan that night was not about his tackling, which the Widnes fans soon came to recognise as much more than adequate, but about the philosophy of the art. Jonathan had fallen into the company of a few Widnes fans representative of the varied types attracted to the game. Brendan McCabe and Derek Burgess run a men's outfitters called Unsworths, and, together with a colleague named John Perrin, occupy a noisy section behind the goal with the arguments continuing in the shop throughout the week. Many is the Widnes player who has popped into Unsworths to buy a pair of trousers and emerged two hours later with his head ringing from a description of every tackle missed and ball dropped for the previous two months.

The point at issue this night, once the pleasantries about the excellence of his second half display had been dispensed, was an incident in the first half when Jonathan was playing full back and he was faced with the situation that full backs dread – an opponent running towards him with the ball and a colleague running alongside him.

Jonathan did exactly what he would have done in union, he moved to meet the man with the ball, keeping his balance and hoping to force his opponent to pass while Jonathan still had time to get to the receiver. But the Hull man delayed his pass until Jonathan was

175

almost on him and sent his colleague away, with Jonathan just failing to dive and tap his heels.

Had he been dealing with a union forward Jonathan would back his chances of bluffing him into parting with the ball earlier so Jonathan could have a good go at the other man but he realised that league forwards are far more adept at running and passing and certainly not as easily forced to act prematurely.

'You should have tackled the man with the ball,' said John, the more insistently argumentative of the Unsworths crowd. But, Jonathan argued, he would still have got the ball away and Jonathan would have had no chance at all of getting the other man.

'Doesn't matter,' said John, 'he might have been selling you a dummy. But whether he was or not, your job was to hit him, and no-one would have blamed you.' Jonathan insisted that when it happened again he would still consider his best chance to stop a try was to stay on his feet until the last moment.

Glyn Shaw, the rugged former Neath and Widnes forward who had been listening with amusement to the argument, explained later: 'It's a different game with different attitudes. If there's a man with the ball, you tackle him. It doesn't matter if he gets rid of it just before you reach him. That's why it is pointless trying to sell a dummy up here, you're going to get hit whether you let go of the ball or not. If you put your man on the deck, they'll forgive you anything.'

It was a small example of the adjustment Jonathan had to make, not only to the new game but to the attitudes of those important people who watch it. But persuading people to watch him was by no means a problem.

His next match was an 'A' team game against local rivals Warrington and once more there was a crowd of around 4000 for the normally neglected Friday night reserve fixture at Naughton Road.

Calculating on the extra 6000 he'd attracted for his debut, the two bumper reserve game gates and the extra thousands put on for the next first team home game against Oldham, Jonathan had repaid £30,000 of his signing-on fee in 22 days. In fact, Widnes were showing a profit, especially in their souvenir shop. Before his arrival they had in stock 2000 replica Widnes shirts which they sold out within a week of his arrival.

But success in rugby league is judged more from the pitch than the balance sheet and Jonathan was making some impressive entries there too. In that second reserve match against Warrington he once more had a shaky start. An attempted touch kick went out on the full instead of bouncing first, even less pardonable in league than it is in union, he missed three goal kicks, and had an attempted kick ahead charged down. The Warrington fans were hooting in derision. Even a conversion he did get went in off a post from right in front.

But in the second half he cut loose again. As if suddenly finding his bearings he put in a couple of decent runs, cracked over a high and confident conversion and then had the crowd roaring with a 60-yard break out of defence. He was roughed up by a couple of tacklers and was awarded a penalty he kicked over to loud cheers. Then he broke the Warrington line with a 30-yard kick ahead which he rapidly pursued, scooping up the bouncing ball without breaking his stride for a spectacular try. At half-time Widnes had been hanging on to a 10–8 lead. In no time at all they were 34–8 ahead and Jonathan was withdrawn from the game to rapturous applause 15 minutes before the end in order to save him for first team duty two days later in a Cup tie at Salford.

Although Widnes had comfortably beaten Salford in Jonathan's introductory game two weeks earlier, it was a much harder game at the Willows and, but for some faulty handling by Salford, Widnes could have been struggling. Jonathan was on the substitutes' bench and, with only about ten minutes to go and Widnes hanging on to a 16–14 lead, Doug sent him on with instructions to get the ball down the Salford end.

Jonathan obliged with a couple of long downfield kicks that were becoming a major contribution to his game as he grappled with the adjustments necessary to the rest of his talents. A penalty goal kicked by Andy Currier finally took the pressure off and Widnes won by 18–14.

The next fixture was a home game against struggling Oldham and an opportunity for Laughton to risk Jonathan for his first full game in the first team, and at stand-off too. It was to be the first subduing experience of his new career, not because he didn't play well but because of the difficulties he found trying to adapt to the ebb and flow of the game at First Division level.

He scored 12 points in all, including a very good try after side-stepping two defenders. Even that magic moment had a snag to it. When league players go over for a try these days they tend not to dive with the ball in their outstretched hands in case they lose their grip before they touch it down. So they clutch it to their chests as they fall. Unfortunately, Jonathan clutched the ball to his stomach.

Spectators thought he was lying there savouring the moment as little boys whooped around him but he had knocked every ounce of wind out of his body.

When the game ended Jonathan came off satisfied with his contribution to a 38–14 victory but physically and mentally exhausted – not by the game or even by being thumped twice in off-the-ball incidents, but by trying to fathom the intricacies of playing stand-off. It was, he concluded, an entirely different role positionally from that in union and the reason he was tired was that he had to run twice as much as necessary trying to get back into the right position before any harm was done.

He had a long and serious talk that night with his team-mates, Alan Tait in particular, about his problems. Tait, as a recent convert from union who had been changed from a union centre to a league full back with brilliant results, felt that centre would be a better position for Jonathan to occupy during his adjustment period.

'Stand-off in league is a position it helps to be born into and it is hard to pick up because it involves an enormous amount of head-on tackling and when you get the ball you usually have forwards to run at,' said Alan.

It was a problem Jonathan was going to have time to ponder because his progress in league was about to slow up considerably as Laughton placed him on the edge of the action as Widnes entered a month of major matches.

▽ J.D.

The Welsh Rugby Union caused a national uproar when they banned me from being interviewed on television at Cardiff Arms Park before the Wales–England International in March 1989. Newspapers and television news programmes were full of the story and 24 MPs signed a motion in the House of Commons condemning the WRU's action.

What the WRU didn't know was that I came very close to suing them for restraint of trade.

I was advised by a solicitor, Frank Nyland of Widnes, that I stood a good chance of getting legal redress for them stopping me earning my living which, now I am a professional sportsman, includes getting paid for appearing on television.

I was so annoyed at the ban I thought long and hard about taking them to court and striking a blow on behalf of all the Welsh rugby league converts through history who've been treated like dirt in their own country. But in the end I thought such an action would make me out to be as petty as the WRU.

The whole affair had blown up without me being aware of it. We had just moved into our new home on the Warrington outskirts and the telephone had yet to be connected. A television crew from BBC Wales came up to record an interview with me and passed on a request to do an interview to camera before and after the international for the Welsh language coverage.

I readily agreed. I'd already received permission from Doug Laughton to miss training that Saturday so that I could be at the match. Wales hadn't lost to England at Cardiff for 26 years and if I couldn't help to stop them this time, at least I wanted to be there to cheer on the lads.

Then a week before the game I read an exclusive story by Peter Jackson in the *Daily Mail* that the WRU secretary David East had told the BBC I would not be allowed to be interviewed on the Arms Park premises.

Apparently the place from which I was going to be interviewed was under the stand in full view of the crowd. David East said although they wished me all the very best and had no feeling of animosity towards me, the request was 'contrary to the International Board rules on amateurism. They make it clear that there can be no promotion or fostering of non-amateur rugby. If Jonathan Davies had been commentating he would have been promoting himself and furthering professional rugby league.'

The press box was full of players who'd professionalised themselves. Why pick on me?

I could hardly believe it. In what way would I have been promoting the league? If I wanted to set up a stall behind the goal, with a sign saying 'Sign Here' and a suitcase full of tenners, they might have had a point. But all I was going to do was talk in Welsh about rugby union. The league wouldn't have been mentioned. Indeed, the very fact I was going to be there was a tribute to the power of Welsh rugby. I would have been paying homage to a great game. I would have been acknowledging that a Welsh international match was an attraction not even a rugby league rebel could resist.

It was all a question of interpretation and the irony was that while the row was even being discussed in Parliament, the French Rugby Union were taking no action over an admission by French coach Pierre Villepreux that he and his Toulouse players were getting paid.

179

So the same rules permitted the French to get paid for playing union, while they debarred me getting paid for talking about it.

I ended up doing the interviews on Canton Bridge surrounded by a big crowd and a lot of publicity. Had the WRU taken no action I doubt if my appearing on Welsh television would have attracted the slightest interest. It was a sad and totally unnecessary episode and all it proved was how out of touch and bewildering the game has become.

I watched the match from the players' box, sitting next to Ieuan Evans's mother and, although I was glad the boys won, I didn't enjoy the pressure on them. I popped in to the Angel Hotel briefly to see the boys and, I must say, the WRU officials I saw were very friendly to me. But I've always found them terrific individually. It is when they get together that they lose touch with reality.

One man I did see was Clive Rowlands, and we were standing quite close to each other when he was asked by a television man if they could interview us together. Clive said he'd prefer not to. He had his reasons I suppose but I had known him and respected him since I was a boy and I would have thought friendship was more important than any other consideration. It upset me.

I had time only for a quick chat at the Angel before Karen picked me up to drive back to Widnes. We had a game at Bradford Northern the following day and I have to say that driving north through the rain when I could have been celebrating another historic win over England was a depressing experience. I swore never to watch Wales at the Arms Park again, at least not until I felt welcome and I could put up with watching the boys under such strain.

When I think of it, that particular stage of my new career was probably the lowest point. Although I had been very pleased with my performance against Warrington a few days before the Wales match, the previous Saturday had been a disaster for Widnes when we were beaten 16–14 in the semi-final of the Challenge Cup by St Helens.

I wasn't playing, and I wasn't even on the substitutes' bench, but I have never felt so shattered and disappointed by a defeat in my life. I couldn't have felt worse if I'd been in a Welsh side that lost to England in Cardiff. If ever a team deserved to get to Wembley it was Widnes but everything that could go wrong, went wrong.

The game was only 10 minutes old when Richie Eyres stuck out his foot, in what was little more than a reflex action, and tripped an opponent. The league had been trying to clamp down on tripping and had given strict instructions to referees to punish any offence with a sending off. Referee John Holdsworth had no hesitation in sending Richie off, not to the sin bin for ten minutes but for the rest of the match. In the 13-a-side game the loss of a forward for 70 minutes is a tremendous disadvantage. The forwards get through between 25 and 30 tackles each, and that's a lot of tackles to be shared around the other 12.

Even so, Widnes nearly pulled it off. We were 14–12 up with just a few minutes left when St Helens mounted a desperate last attack down the left and Les Quirk wriggled through for a try.

I felt more disappointed for Doug and the boys than I did for myself. I must admit I fancied a chance of playing at Wembley but the team had earned the right to be there with some wonderful performances in the earlier rounds when the draw gave them three very tough away fixtures.

What made the depression even worse was the opportunity it gave to the St Helens coach Alex Murphy to do some high profile crowing – something he is very good at. I don't dislike Alex, he was a great player and he's the sort of colourful character who takes as much abuse as he gives, but he did get on my nerves.

When I signed for Widnes, Alex immediately began ranting and raving about how I had promised to sign for them when I came back from the Lions tour. He said we had shaken hands on a deal.

It is about time I put the record straight on that one. I have never discussed personally with Alex any move to St Helens. I had met him twice prior to signing for Widnes, once after a Llanelli–Neath match and the other when I called to see Stuart Evans at St Helens when I was on a course in Liverpool. Neither time did we talk about any sort of deal. When I had my meetings with St Helens in the summer of 1988 I dealt solely with their chairman Joe Pickavance. I also met members of the St Helens committee. Alex must have been away because he didn't figure in the negotiations at all.

When I decided not to accept their offer we left it that they would try again after the Lions tour. At Christmas, when the rumours about Widnes's interest were flying around, Joe Pickavance rang me at home. I said, truthfully, that I had no intention of signing for anyone.

Then the sequence of events I have described elsewhere fell into place and I found myself a Widnes player. On the day I signed, St Helens spoke to Karen and offered to increase their offer yet again.

I am sorry if St Helens were upset and sorry, too, for Leeds who were the first to make me a firm offer two years earlier. But you can only sign for one club.

Perhaps if Alex had taken the trouble to visit me in Wales and sell me his club and the game as eloquently as Doug and Jim Mills did, I would have been a St Helens player. But he didn't, and he can't even say I was holding out for more money. But Alex had missed out on a few signings and accusing me of two-timing him was probably his way of avoiding criticism. It got so bad at one stage that Doug hit back in the press and suggested that next time Alex wanted to buy a union man he, Doug, would do the business for him.

That kept Alex quiet for a while but when, after my first few appearances, Doug began to keep me out of the big matches Alex started up again, saying I was being wasted. One of the sad features I've found in league is the way top coaches have a go at each other in the press. They should let their results do the talking.

One of the reasons I joined Widnes was Doug's promise that he would introduce me slowly, giving me plenty of time to adjust. He could make that promise because Widnes were the best team in the League whether I was in it or not. After we won at Salford in the Cup, we were drawn away to Castleford who were top of the League at that time and going great guns. I was on the bench in that tie and could only marvel along with the rest of the country as the boys tore Castleford apart in the first half. We were 22–0 up in 15 minutes – some said it was the best burst of rugby they'd ever seen. I got on for a few minutes at the end but the game was as good as over.

Then we had the bad luck to be drawn away to Leeds in the quarter final and Doug decided to leave me out of the game completely. I was disappointed but I could see his point. Why play someone who was still green when the team were going like a train? Leeds were duly beaten 24–4 and when St Helens came out of the hat with us for the semi-final, Doug reasoned that he ought to keep faith with the same team. Once again, I felt sad at not playing but I never once questioned Doug's judgement. When you get left out by a selection committee you don't respect you tend to feel aggrieved. But when one man you trust does it, a man whose livelihood and reputation depends on his decisions, you quickly come to terms with it.

Murphy had been on before the match about me not playing,

afterwards he was excitably claiming he would never have left me out. Others said I might have made the difference. They may or may not be right, but one thing I am sure about, had I played and Widnes still lost, they would have been queuing up to say what a waste of money I'd been – and Alex would have been at the head of them.

Nevertheless, it was a disappointing time but I was not out of the action for long. Widnes were about to enter a period of 10 games in 32 days that would determine if they could retain the Championship and it was all hands on deck.

A match at Bradford, played in terribly muddy conditions, proved how hard that task was going to be and we struggled to a 16–16 draw.

The following Wednesday we faced a game at Oldham who were fighting to avoid relegation and were sure to give us another hard game. I was in the side at stand-off and one of the reasons I remember the day so well is that it was the day the Lions squad to tour Australia was announced.

I know I had turned my back on all that but as I heard the names being read out on the radio I couldn't suppress a feeling of sadness. More immediately I was upset because brother-in-law Phil hadn't been chosen. But I have to confess that beneath my disappointment on his behalf, I was feeling pretty sick myself for the death of one of my great ambitions. Perhaps I wouldn't have been captain as once I'd hoped but I would have been there. After I signed for Widnes the Lions coach Ian McGeechan had said how disappointed he was because he had been building the Lions strategy around me. It is a pity he didn't tell me that before.

I remember reading about the Lions squad in the paper as the team coach drove towards Oldham. It was a filthy night, snow and hail beat against the window and it was freezing cold. But it was no good thinking of sunny Australia – my life was more concerned with doing the business on a dirty night in Oldham.

Perhaps it was then that the reality of my new life took me over completely. All I know is I went out onto that snow covered, windswept pitch determined to have a good game and stuff a few words down a few throats.

For the first time since I'd gone north I felt as if I had some control over the proceedings, like the old days. I scored two tries, each from about 60 yards, kicked five goals and a drop goal for a total of 19 points. We won 35–16 and I enjoyed every minute.

Doug was full of praise and the newspapers the following day made encouraging reading. In his column in the *Daily Mirror* Alex Murphy was off again. He wrote, 'When Jonathan Davies showed what we already knew he could do – ripping Oldham to shreds on his own – he did his Widnes coach Doug Laughton no favours . . . who knows, Widnes might have been at Wembley instead of us if Doug had taken what would have been no gamble at all on Jonathan's instinctive match winning skills.' He couldn't let the subject drop.

Oddly enough, our next game was away to St Helens and I've rarely looked forward to a match so much. In fact, the entire team were out for revenge that day; we got it in style, winning 44–16 and thereby inflicting the heaviest home defeat in the League that St Helens have suffered since the war.

The people on our bench could distinctly hear a voice from the St Helens bench shouting, 'Get that Welsh bastard.' But they couldn't make out who it was.

As a matter of fact I did get clobbered a few times. Paul Loughlin got penalised for a late tackle on me and Shane Cooper tried to strangle me but they didn't manage to prevent me from scoring a try and kicking eight goals for 20 points.

I'll allow the irrepressible Alex to have the last word. In his column in the *Daily Mirror* he wrote about how we'd met a few days before the match and he'd told me not to forget to turn up. He was sorry he had reminded me. 'He murdered us on his own,' he said.

17
Hard-won Medals

The home dressing room at Naughton Park, Widnes, has few luxury refinements. It is on the small side and basic, and it is surprising to find a copy of Rudyard Kipling's 'If', written in black on a gold-painted metal plaque, rusting quietly on one wall. I hadn't realised before that the line 'If you can keep your head . . . ' referred to rugby league.

The battered wooden benches and lockers are due for retirement and the deep communal bath probably looks inviting only after a hard game. It was here that Jonathan first revealed the torso that made the physiotherapist laugh but which gathered respect quicker than it accumulated the extra muscle they said he would need to comply with the demands of his new calling.

As a dressing room it is not a lot worse than most in which the gladiators of our winter ball games prepare and recover from the action. I suspect, however, that the guardians of the league game's tradition prefer to retain the spartan touch.

The engaging Eddie McDonnell, the club's chief scout, is in charge of dressing preparations such as rubbing down, performed by the substitutes, and the taping-up of ankles, wrists and thumb joints. He also administers first aid, a devotion which leads to oaths Hippocrates would probably not recognise.

After his first full match against Oldham, Jonathan found himself not only physically and mentally shattered but suffering from more cuts and scrapes about the legs and knees than he had ever sustained in union. The increased activity involved in the extra amount of tackling and being tackled in league plays havoc with unprotected and unseasoned flesh.

185

'Hang on, Jonathan,' said Eddie, 'I'll get you something for those cuts.' So Jonathan sat around contemplating his battered legs and, after a while, noticed that his team-mates were not hurrying to get to the bar as they normally do. The Hulme brothers, David and Paul, in particular were sitting there fully dressed and smiling at him.

Then Eddie came back into the room bearing a large bottle of iodine which he proceeded to pour over Jonathan's legs. The resulting squeals were ample reward for the patience of his colleagues.

Now Jonathan dresses quickly to hide the cuts and grass burns, and when Eddie wanders around asking 'any cuts lads?', he joins the chorus denying any need for treatment.

Jonathan found the atmosphere of the dressing room different to that of union – much quieter and more matter-of-fact, with fewer examples of players psyching up themselves and their colleagues. He is very conscious of the team feeling at Widnes but each player is responsible for his own temperamental contribution to it and there's less of the air-punching bravado that passes for team spirit in many dressing rooms. At first he found the lack of obvious camaraderie difficult mainly because he was not privy to the in-jokes and the nicknames. The use of sometimes obscure nicknames is common to all sportsmen and often amounts to a private language that a new-comer has to learn the hard way.

Jonathan's nickname in Welsh rugby circles was 'Jiffy' for a reason he has never fathomed. When the same name was chosen for a brand of condoms he tended to discourage it, but it is still what he answers to when he meets his former Welsh team-mates.

His christening in league came during a practice match. He was playing full back and when a high ball was hoisted he decided to take full responsibility for it and screeched 'JD's ball' in a high pitched voice that had the other Widnes players falling about with laughter. He has been called JD ever since, and whenever a high ball goes up during a match you may hear a few falsetto voices call mockingly 'JD's ball'.

But that sort of banter will not leave him lacking in response. He's protected by a sharp wit and a quick delivery and, not for the first time, an ability to prove himself among bigger men and in a sport for which he is too easily dismissed as physically unsuited.

If Doug Laughton needed any final convincing about Jonathan's ability to fulfil his quota of hard tackling he got it from watching him set about the All Blacks. But not everybody saw that display and some might have even doubted its relevance to the almost continuous necessity for a league player to be ready to stop an opponent in his tracks. Neither is bravery the complete answer to a convert's problems in this respect because there is a basic difference in the way a tackler has to align himself. And it was this initial period of adjustment that led some to persist in questioning Jonathan's ability to turn in an acceptable workload of grounded foes.

He sought advice from his team-mates. Doug warned him about trying to stop the really big men by taking them head-on. 'Let them go past and grab something as they do,' he told him. Martin Offiah, who admits to scoring more tries than he makes tackles, has become adept at catching hold of part of an opponent and hanging on grimly.

Jonathan finds the method convenient at times although his new found friend and golf coach Mike Nicholas, the former Aberavon, Warrington and Great Britain forward, says that Jonathan's tackling often reminds him of a cowboy trying to wrestle a steer in a rodeo.

Alan Tait, the former union back who experienced the same problem when he arrived the previous season, describes how he dealt with his first big tackling test. 'I suddenly found myself guarding our line as a 17-stone forward charged towards me. He had a man outside him and all he had to do was pass and a try was certain. But he came trundling on, his eyes fixed on mine, and I realised he was intending to run right through me. I braced myself and just before the impact I went down on my haunches, grabbed him around the legs and went back with him. He came crashing down and they didn't get a try.'

It is another method that Jonathan had added to his list of felling options but the most telling part of his tackling is the number of times during a match he effectively stops the opposition.

Widnes supporters were finally persuaded of this in the home match against Warrington, their local rivals in March. This is invariably the toughest match of the year, home or away, because of the feelings between the clubs and supporters and the corresponding match the previous season had ended in a bit of a riot.

The game took place a few days after the disappointing semi-final defeat by St Helens and Widnes were badly in need of a boost to their morale. Jonathan, who had not played a full match for over five weeks, was in similar need.

He was chosen to play at left centre with Martin Offiah outside him. On the opposite flank were Darren Wright and Andy Currier who normally partner each other in the centre.

It was a three-quarter line that raised a few eyebrows, not least in the Warrington dressing room. The Wright–Currier partnership on the right looked capable enough. They are both tall, fast and strong in attack and difficult for the other side to get past.

But while Jonathan and Martin had everything going for them in attacking pace it looked very much a flank that could be fragile in defence. Doug Laughton was about to submit his two union stars to a fierce test.

Warrington didn't need any further invitation and directed most of their traffic down the right. Jonathan found himself under early pressure and drew applause when he caught and tackled a swiftly breaking Des Drummond. It was a good start that the pair success-fully built on. Martin scored five tries in the 32–4 victory, three of them assisted by Jonathan who made 12 tackles, an impressive number for a back. Warrington's only try came down the other flank. Jonathan was twice fouled off the ball and proved beyond doubt his ability to withstand the demands and rigours of a hard fought match. It was a reputation he went on improving until the end of the season.

▽ J.D.

When I took my first nervous steps into rugby league I was so scared the only medal I thought I might qualify for was the Victoria Cross. Exactly four months later I emerged from the end of the season with a Championship winner's medal and a Premiership winner's medal. I'd played 12 full games and scored 105 points and, apart from a few dents and scratches, I was unscathed.

But most of all, I had passed the first hurdle of acceptance as a rugby league player. Rival fans still shouted, 'Get your nose onside, Davies' but they no longer doubted the physical commitment I was able to give to the game – and that was important to me, as it has been all my life.

I was still a long way from being the player I wanted to be. I was still well short of the creative standards I achieved in union, but even the most optimistic judges said it would take me at least a season to adapt my skills to the new discipline. But at least I had had firsthand experience of the club game at the highest level – not Wembley maybe, but the next best thing.

The Premiership final at Old Trafford ends the season in a flourish, with both the Second and First Division finals played on the same day. The Premiership involves the top eight teams in the division playing on a knockout basis and if things had gone to plan we would have played Wigan in the final.

We ought to have met Wigan at Wembley but that controversial sending-off cost us the semi-final against St Helens who went on to fall so easily to Wigan in the final that it was spoiled as a spectacle.

But the fans still had two Widnes–Wigan clashes to look forward to. Wigan had beaten us in the John Player Special Trophy a couple of days after I'd signed and so were on target to win all four big titles. Having been knocked out of the Cup and beginning to feel the strain of a fixture pile-up that forced us to play a match every three days, Widnes lost successive matches against Bradford and Hull. The Championship, that had looked ours for the taking, now hinged on the last game of the season – at home to Wigan.

It was all-ticket admission and the 16,000 crowd could have been easily doubled if Widnes had agreed to take the match to Everton's ground at Goodison Park. But the Widnes committee reckoned they owed it to their faithful fans to play the game at Naughton Park and I was delighted. It is not the grandest ground in the world but it's a great place to play rugby and have it appreciated.

Our fans certainly appreciated that night, once they'd got over the shock we gave them at the start when we let Wigan through for a try in the first minute. I then proceeded to miss two penalties and a conversion. None of them was from an easy position but I should have got at least one. But as it was Wigan took their lead to 12–4 before Martin scored and I converted just before half-time to make it 10–12. One of my few consolations was that I brought down the big New Zealander Adrian Shelford – it might have made him feel better if he'd known I'd done the same to his cousin Wayne the previous year.

In the second half we just cut loose and although we had Emosi Koloto sent off we finished up winning 32–18. I believe it was the hardest game of rugby I'd ever played in my life. The pace and commitment never let up for a second. I'd had a torn thigh muscle for a few weeks and I shouldn't have played but I was only one of a half dozen players on either side who carried an injury into the match. It was the sort of game you'd need a death certificate to get excused from. But despite the injuries nobody let up and, of course, we finished feeling a lot healthier because we won the Championship.

Widnes have no proper committee box so they erect a temporary structure out of scaffolding and planks at the club-house end of the ground. I've been on posher podiums but never one as exciting as this as the Widnes fans crammed into that end of the ground. We took it in turns to wave the trophy at them. They weren't satisfied until we'd taken our shirts off and thrown them into the crowd.

We had a good drink in the social club and then went off to the Hillcrest for a victory dinner. I had some friends up from Wales who were surprised that our celebrations were so subdued. I tried to explain that we were deliriously happy but we were too knackered to do anything else but sit and drink. Big games in rugby league, and most of them tend to be big, drag every ounce of energy and effort out of you.

Winning the Championship made up for the disappointment of the Cup and brought up the prospect of Widnes meeting Wigan in the Premiership final to settle who was the better team. But Wigan did the last thing anyone expected – they lost 4–2 to St Helens. It was the week before they were due to meet at Wembley but there was no excuse. St Helens had upset the apple-cart again.

Saints then had to meet us in the Premiership semi-final on a very hot day and a bone hard pitch that was just made for our pace; we beat them 38–14. That meant we were to meet Hull in the final at Old Trafford. Since Hull had beaten us 23–16 a few weeks before, it was a chance to do a bit of tidying up before the end of the season. Their coach Brian Smith had done a fabulous job to rescue them from the bottom of the League but we felt he'd gone a little too far when he told the press that we had an inflated view of our abilities.

The press also made great play of the fact that Gary Pearce, my predecessor at Llanelli, had outshone me, scoring 18 points to my 12. As it happened Gary did play well. After two difficult years following his move to Hull, he had suddenly found his feet and was really in dominating form. We allowed him too much room thinking he didn't have the pace and he did a lot of damage.

The chance of getting even, therefore, added a lot to the game but, quite honestly, the atmosphere at Old Trafford that day was incentive enough. The crowd was a record of over 40,000 and although they weren't as noisy as the Arms Park's 60,000, the atmosphere was fantastic. But there was one big difference – the intensity. When I've played at the Arms Park for Wales, or even for my club, the feeling of tension is tremendous. It is a great pressure to have to bear. You would think that in a professional game like league the tension would be even greater but it isn't.

At Old Trafford that day the will to win was as fierce as ever but the atmosphere was one of celebration, as if the important thing was to produce a great day for rugby. I really didn't feel any of the pressure I used to feel at Cardiff, I just felt I wanted to play good rugby and enjoy the occasion.

The result was a terrific game and enjoyable experience. Hull fought like tigers throughout. I hear they had been giving their tackling bags such a hammering in training that week they'd torn them to shreds. It certainly felt like it. But they had no answer to our pace. Darren Wright ran 70 yards for the first try. I had a try disallowed for offside, which was a borderline decision if I may say so. Then Andy Currier ran 95 yards for our second try. I ran with him all the way in case he felt like passing, which he didn't. Although we lost Joe Grima to the sin bin in the first half, we coped pretty well. There were some great handling movements but we just couldn't subdue them enough to put on a show. Gary and I scored six points each, so I suppose honours were even in that direction, but he played a commanding game at stand-off while I was on the wing, hardly getting a pass but making my contribution with 11 tackles.

It was a triumph which confirmed what a very good idea it was to join Widnes. They are truly a great side. It is like playing for Wales every week, but while Wales sometimes have players who aren't quite up to it, Widnes never do.

When you think of the task I faced when I arrived, it is amazing I got in the side at all. I arrived as a stand-off to find that in Tony Myler they had the best in Britain. He breaks his ankle and David Hulme takes his place and wins the Rugby League Player of the Year title. David's brother Paul, who played hooker for Great Britain, takes over as scrum-half like a champion. The centres Wright and Currier are among the best in the country. On one wing you have Rick Thackray and on the other Martin Offiah who is the fastest player I've ever seen.

Has a rugby union convert ever had such a standard to live up to? First they sign Martin who had broken every record there was to break in his first 18 months. Then they sign Alan Tait from Kelso who gets into the Great Britain team in no time at all and who in that Premiership final won the Man of the Match award. And Emosi Koloto comes over from Tonga, having barely heard of rugby league, to establish himself as an international class second row in his first season.

And in addition you have players like Mike O'Neill, the second row who was playing in his fifth Premiership since 1980 and was still able to play magnificently on the wing when we had injuries in the final. Phil McKenzie, the hooker, can run and kick better than most backs, Kurt Sorensen is rated the best forward in the world on his day, Joe Grima and Derek Pyke can tackle like tanks and set up attacks with subtle little passes, while loose forward Richard Eyres always seems in the running for the Man of the Match award. Barry Dowd can step into almost any position on the field and David Myers made his debut at 17 against Oldham and scored a hat-trick of tries.

To play, let alone shine, among that lot I faced a new season in which I was going to have to find a way to achieve the same control of the game I had gained in union. But in union I was aware of everything and everybody on the field. I could make up my mind to do something so quickly I was gone before even I knew it, never mind the opposition.

But it was taking a long time for me to attain that awareness in league. I was having to think for that split second longer – and they are on to you so quickly in league you have even less time to think. Only at the scrum does a stand-off get the same time and space as he does in union. But the scrums are such a shambles, you rarely get a clean ball.

Neither are they as easily fooled. They don't take dummies, they take you. I used to have a tactic in union where I would run across our three-quarter line shaping to pass, but keeping the ball in my outstretched hand. I could do this two or three times and leave a few confused opponents behind. I tried it against St Helens one day. Three times I made as if to pass and drew the ball back in the last minute. Then I looked up and found I still had the three opponents with me and ready to pounce.

I am sure it will come but I know it won't come quickly. I felt I was also going to have to say my piece a little more vigorously. In union I had the habit of telling everyone what to do, what tactic to look out for. And I was respected enough to be listened to.

In league I didn't feel like contributing until I was sure of my ground. But I do like to have my say, to argue everything through and take responsibility for trying new ideas.

One of the encouraging things that has happened since I arrived in league is that they are thinking of introducing a World Rugby League Sevens championship. Now, I don't see how there can be a lot of difference from union sevens. I could pick a team from Widnes that could challenge any sevens team in the world in either code. Come to think of it, I could probably pick two.

Sevens rugby is how I first made my mark in union and perhaps it'll help get me into the swing of things in league. It is going to be a battle to get to the top, but that's what I came north to do. It is already obvious that I've joined the top club. Friendly players, fantastic support and great rugby is all a man can ask for.

18
Honest Rugby

As the chronicler of Jonathan's thoughts and deeds in the year or so leading up to and beyond his sudden decision to turn to rugby league I am conscious most of all that this story isn't over yet.

Usually one waits until the end of a sporting career before embarking on a description of it and hindsight can be a sturdy ally in those circumstances. But having decided to write about a career as it was happening, I found myself caught up in the middle of a dilemma that doesn't often happen elsewhere in sport – or life, for that matter. Many of us find ourselves torn by a career decision but not often is that decision irrevocable, involving a change of job description and of a philosophy and carrying a considerable risk of humiliating failure.

The way Jonathan was virtually forced into that decision by the hamfistedness of the Welsh Rugby Union made me resentful. As a Welshman and a fan, if not a devotee, of rugby union I wanted to see him in the Five Nations Championship, and then on the British Lions tour of Australia and then facing up to the All Blacks in Wales.

In place of that itinerary I found myself at Naughton Park and unexotic places to the north and east. The profound alarm he felt at the consequences of his decision and the intolerable pressure applied on him in his first couple of weeks was felt strongly by those around him. It was a nervy time but in watching him pick his way through it, a new regard and affection for rugby league as a game developed.

He was certainly not ostracised by union as he feared. He received almost 200 messages of good wishes and goodwill from union men all over the world, including an amusing begging letter from Nigel

Carr, the Irish flanker! The ban on his appearance on television at the Arms Park and the subsequent dithering about whether he, Paul Moriarty and Adrian Hadley should be invited to a lunch to celebrate the previous year's Triple Crown win – in which all three had played a major part – seemed trivial in comparison.

And his welcome in league was genuine, even though league followers have a defiant, almost siege-like, love for their game and often wish to see the odd union star fail to make the grade to confirm their belief in its superiority. One area of the game's reputation they are particularly jealous of is tackling, the fierceness of which they are justly proud. I once suggested that when there isn't a match they pop down to the M6 to watch the car crashes, but my comment wasn't appreciated.

Jonathan was on the bench in a match at Featherstone who were giving Widnes a bit of a battering which they eventually overcame. Three old ladies sitting in front of me were shouting, 'Get Davies on, Laughton. Take t'cotton wool off him.' The mood of the place indicated that it would have been the modern equivalent of throwing someone to the lions, and Laughton wisely paid no heed.

He explained later, 'Jonathan was bought for the long term. Too many union men have been thrown straight into the action in average teams and suffered either physically or mentally as a result. As it was, our fixture pile-up forced me to play him regularly after a couple of months and he did exceptionally well. We had a spell of ten games in 32 days and he played in eight and a half of them. It confirmed that he is going to be a great success.'

That success was far from guaranteed at first in the minds of most of the league fraternity. When Jonathan was signed, David Berry of the *South Wales Echo* conducted a poll of all coaches in the First Division of the Rugby League, asking if they would have spent a world record fee on Jonathan. Only Alex Murphy said he would – the other 12 replied bluntly that they would have found better ways of spending the money.

But something else was at stake besides the careers of those concerned – the attitude of Welsh players to league. Wales has long been a fertile hunting ground for the professional game – Jonathan was the 154th Welsh international to make the change – but injuries to Terry Holmes and David Bishop and the lack of immediate success experienced by Stuart Evans, Gary Pearce and Adrian Hadley had reduced the temptation significantly. Had Jonathan been splattered or if he had failed, the temptation might have disappeared altogether.

But his progress has opened gates that will take some closing. Paul Moriarty and Jonathan Griffiths had other reasons prompting them to follow him north, but there's no doubt his experience increased their appetite. In Moriarty's case the link was stronger. The sharply increased attendances that followed Jonathan's arrival not only paid off Widnes's £30,000 down payment to him, but improved the club's cash flow to such an extent that ten weeks later they were able to offer Moriarty an estimated £100,000 fee. Moriarty had long had his eye on the prospects available in league and admits that his firsthand view of the way Jonathan had been received into the game had helped form his decision.

Jonathan Griffiths, who was Jonathan's half back partner at Llanelli, also admitted that seeing how his former colleague had fared helped him to decide to accept the offer from St Helens. Welsh rugby was paying a high price for its poor handling of the young men under its control.

In assessing the effect of Jonathan's departure – in addition to paving the way for others like Moriarty and Griffiths – I asked Clem Thomas to weigh up his loss. 'It will be a while before the Welsh know what they've lost,' he said. 'He played behind the worst pack in living memory and when you achieve what he achieved under those circumstances, you must be a great player. Game after game he was trying to win from set-piece possession and that's a brave thing to try. He worked miracles and I don't know when we will again see anyone conjure a try out of thin air like he did.'

Those of us who were waiting for him to do the same in league have had to be patient. There's not much thin air about in that game. But he has destroyed the myth that he can't tackle. He was soon contributing over ten a game, which is good going for a back. And his kicking was soon established as a major plus.

As he fights now to establish his credentials as a creative force in league he will no doubt keep us on edge as he always did in union never knowing what he is going to try next.

And no doubt he will still have too much to say for himself, particularly about the union game he has left behind. I asked him once to compare how other players in union would take to league and vice versa.

He said: 'I often think of players I've played with in union and those I'm now with in league and I can't see them other than as rugby players. I know the games are different, but that's what they are – just rugby players.'

But that is precisely what they are not allowed to be. It's a shame – more than that, it is a crime.

▽ J.D.

I have long resented the hypocrisy in rugby union, for their continual insistence that the game is amateur when it obviously isn't. But I've come to resent it even more since I moved to rugby league.

Not just because I've left behind a number of union players all over the world who openly earn a good living from the game without the mental and physical upheaval I, and many like me, have undergone – but because I've found myself among a group of sportsmen who suffer more discrimination than any others in the whole world of sport.

When I was a union player I saw the matter purely and simply as a conflict about being able to make money out of being a good rugby player. Since my move I realise it goes a lot deeper, and is a lot more sinister, than that. It is rugby league that union wages its war against, not professionalism as such. The rift between the two codes may be nearly 100 years old but the hatred is still as strong, particularly from the union side. And the rugby league player bears the biggest brunt of it.

The image persists of league players as a bunch of northern toughies who bash each other senseless for the sake of a few quid every week. In sharp contrast, the union men down south are presented as clean-cut, well-educated middle-class heroes who want no more return from their rugger than a ripping good game and a jolly old sing-song in the bar afterwards.

The images are based on the totally false impression that one game is played for money, and the other for fun.

If anyone had the choice of being born with a brilliant talent for rugby in the middle of Wigan or in the stockbroker belt of Surrey, there is not much doubt where his rugby ability would be worth the most money. The top class union player who goes to the right school and the right university needn't be too bright to be guaranteed a well-paid and comfortable life, living off his rugby fame.

Although more lucrative opportunities are creeping into rugby league, the top home-grown player is still unlikely to earn much over £10,000 a year to go with his earnings from his regular job which is not usually comparable with the big-money employment available to union players.

197

There is no basis for denouncing league as an out-and-out professional game, any more than there is for declaring union to be a purely amateur pursuit.

But the penalty inflicted on a man brought up to be a rugby league player has nothing to do with money, it is to do with discrimination. He is denied a right that exists for any other sportsman who gets paid – professionals from soccer, American football, snooker, tennis, golf or any sport you care to mention can elect to play rugby union tomorrow. But a rugby league man can't. He can't even do what I've done and change codes.

My rugby league colleagues at Widnes and most of the others I've met are not all that fond of rugby union, anyway. But I'm sure they must be as curious about what it is like to play union as I was about league. And I'm sure that many of them are good enough rugby players, not only to make the change but play at international level as well although they would probably find the transformation as difficult as I've done at first.

It doesn't apply to Wales, Scotland or Ireland, but in England it is hard to accept that a group of rugby players are doomed by reason of their birthplace never to be allowed to represent their country at Twickenham.

Supposing Ellery Hanley or Tony Myler, or any of the great rugby players in league at the moment, were to wake up one morning to find themselves with the burning ambition to play rugby union for their country. What human or moral right has anyone got to stop them giving up their league wages and joining a union club?

The RFU might well claim the right to be the sole judges about who should play their game. But they don't own England do they? They might be empowered to decide who is good enough to play for England – but what law gives them the power to decide which Englishmen are entitled to play?

Billy Boston had a tremendous league career at Wigan, leaving Cardiff as a teenager after being told he would never play for Cardiff RFC, and probably not Wales either because of his colour. He found a real welcome among people who are discriminated against because of their sport if not their colour.

Most rugby players in Britain, whatever their code, are treated badly by the union authorities who seem to regard the game as their private club, the best privileges of which are extended only to a favoured few. The others, including the poor and uneducated like me, have to muddle through as best they can. I can't imagine why the Welsh Rugby Union allow themselves to be ruled by the same philosophy when they haven't even got the old school tie as an excuse.

The tragedy is that the two codes have so much to learn from each other. I considered I would be a much better union player after only four months in league. And I can see how league players could benefit from a spell in union. They are different games and would keep their separate identities, even if players were allowed to switch between the two.

I knew what I was doing. I knew I was burning my bridges. But I still harbour a secret dream that one day I will play union again. The chances are pretty slim considering the fuss over my going. But why shouldn't Martin Offiah be allowed to play for England if he wants to? His union career had barely started when he went north. It would be great to see him in action at Twickenham. English rugby fans wouldn't be disappointed either – particularly if he was playing outside Hanley.

In the summer of 1989 John Stewart, a New Zealand RFU councillor, called for players to be allowed to set up trust funds for when they retired. If the International Rugby Union didn't agree with it, he said, New Zealand should leave it and play rugby with someone else. If countries like Wales and France did the same, the world of rugby union would begin to look a lot different. Old pros like me might even get recalled for international duty! I would have given a lot to have been out in Australia with the British Lions last summer. While it was going on I felt so sad at not being there I telephoned Ieuan Evans to find out what it was like. It was home-sickness in reverse. It's an odd feeling I fear others will exerience.

Certainly the number of Welshmen tempted to take the northern trail must be worrying. Losing Paul Moriarty and Jonathan Griffiths were sad blows.

I noticed that David East, the secretary of the WRU, complained at the time of Jonathan Griffith's move that Jonathan had been discourteous in not informing them he was going to St Helens when he should have been at a Welsh squad session. When I think of the almost complete lack of courtesy shown to players by the Welsh RU over the years, Jonathan is easily forgiven. Stories of bad treatment of players are rife throughout the game and are the foundation of most of the dissatisfaction that forces a player to consider pulling up his roots and moving to another game.

Paul Moriarty, who had done great service for Wales in 23 internationals, was told he would never play for Wales again. Where's the courtesy in that, telling a 24-year-old that his remaining ambitions are useless? Not because he had done anything wrong but because his face didn't fit any longer. I think Paul will have a great career at Widnes and will be able to get the rugby satisfaction he was denied in Wales.

Jonathan Griffiths was my half back partner at Llanelli and is not only an excellent player but an intelligent, sensible young man who has got a lot to offer any sport. He played in the Welsh team against Scotland in January, the first one I missed after my move to Widnes, and struggled to make good use of a lot of messy ball. I said to myself as I watched the game on television, 'They've got another Jonathan to make a scapegoat.' Sure enough, he took the stick and he was dropped for the next match and when his name didn't come up in the Lions squad what was there left for him? Wales can't go on losing players of this calibre. Not everyone can play for Wales but they can be treated properly and included in planning.

Paul and Jonathan will join a new organisation in league – the Association of Welsh Rugby League Players. It is an idea thought up mainly by Jim Mills and David Watkins. I went to the inaugural meeting. It was fascinating to meet some of the great names who had preceded me, like Lewis Jones and Billy Boston. In many ways they had it tougher than me in that they were ostracised when they went back to their own country. I might have had more pressure on me because of the money but at least I'm still welcome at Trimsaran and Llanelli.

Mike Nicholas, who was thrown out of the Aberavon clubhouse when he went back after signing for Warrington, looked around the gathering and said, 'It is like a meeting of the PLO, we haven't got a homeland.' It was more of a sad than a bitter comment, made on behalf of men who feel cut off from the birthplace of their sporting careers. It is significant that so many have remained up north after their playing days were over.

Perhaps I haven't been away long enough to get that nostalgic but I certainly don't have a regret in the world. I might find fault with the attitudes in the game I've left behind, but I have many happy memories of union and many friends I hope I won't lose. Having said that, I'm proud to be a member of that body of men who risked all for their belief that there's nothing wrong in a man earning a living from his skill. It is a hard decision but it is an honest one.

I comforted myself in those hectic early days in league by working out when I would play my last match for Widnes. Now I don't care when that is – as long as it's far, far away.

Index

Index